Poetic Remedies

Torn Curtain Publishing
Wellington, New Zealand
www.torncurtainpublishing.com

© Copyright 2023 Penelope J. Kern. All rights reserved.

ISBN Softcover 978-0-473-68439-6
ISBN EPub 978-0-473-68440-2

This book is not intended as a substitute for professional counselling, or medical advice, or treatment.

No portion of this book may be reproduced, stored in a retrieval system or transmitted in any form or by any means—electronic, mechanical, photocopy, recording or otherwise—except for brief quotations in printed reviews or promotion, without prior written permission from the author.

Unless otherwise noted, all scripture is taken from the New Living Translation, NLT. Copyright © 1996, 2004, 2015 by Tyndale House Foundation. Used by permission of Tyndale House Publishers, Inc., Carol Stream, Illinois 60188. All rights reserved.

Scripture quotations marked TPT are from The Passion Translation®. Copyright © 2017, 2018 by Passion & Fire Ministries, Inc. Used by permission. All rights reserved. ThePassionTranslation.com.

Scripture quotations marked NKJV are taken from the New King James Version. Copyright © 1982 by Thomas Nelson, Inc. Used by permission. All rights reserved.

Scripture quotations marked AMP are taken from the Amplified® Bible (AMPC), Copyright © 1954, 1958, 1962, 1964, 1965, 1987 by The Lockman Foundation. Used by permission. www.lockman.org.

Scripture quotations marked ESV are from the The Holy Bible, English Standard Version®, copyright © 2001 by Crossway, a publishing ministry of Good News Publishers. Used by permission. All rights reserved.

Scripture quotations marked NIV are from the Holy Bible, New International Version®, copyright © 1973, 1978, 1984, 2011 by Biblica, Inc.™ Used by permission of Zondervan. All rights reserved worldwide.

Scripture quotations marked KJV are taken from The Authorized (King James) Version. Rights in the Authorized Version in the United Kingdom are vested in the Crown. Reproduced by permission of the Crown's patentee, Cambridge University Press.

Illustrations by @nur.adil88. Used with permission.

Cataloguing in Publishing Data
Title: Poetic Remedies: Joy-Infused Healing for Your Mind, Emotions, Spirit and Body
Author: Penelope J. Kern
Subjects: Inspirational & religious poetry; body, mind & spirit; mental health; physical health; wholeness and healing; humorous poetry; health and wellbeing; Christian living.

A copy of this title is held at the National Library of New Zealand.

Poetic Remedies

JOY-INFUSED HEALING FOR YOUR MIND,
EMOTIONS, SPIRIT AND BODY

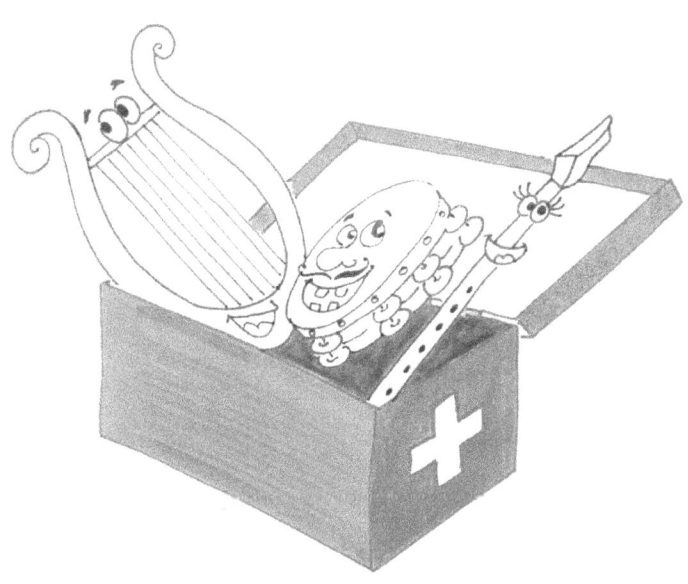

Penelope J. Kern

Penelope's book, *Poetic Remedies*, is written with such anointed tenderness! There is something in the word-songs that she has created that give them life of their own, swirling and moving to a divine dance. It's the very breath of the Holy Spirit upon them! Her poems have a way of releasing the presence of heaven into the atmosphere. As you read them, you can literally breathe them in deeply. Thank you, Penelope! This book is going to bring great healing, comfort, freedom and peace to those who choose to let their souls be captivated by the wonder of what you have written.

Gabby Conlon
Deputy Director, School of Faith
Melbourne, Australia

Penelope Kern has written a book that is both beautiful and powerful. Anointed words based on scripture are woven into poetry. However, these poems are not mere flowery verses. Oh, no! They are directives from the Word of God brilliantly coded into rhyme and blank verse.

Use these poems to bolster your faith as you walk out your healing, prosperity, breakthrough, or whatever promise from the Lord you believe you receive (Mark 11:24). Penelope, thank you for sharing your unique and timely gifts with the Body of Christ.

Dr. Laurette Willis
Founder of *PraiseMoves*, Christian Life Coach and Author
Oklahoma, USA

Penelope's friendship with Jesus always inspires me. Her boldness to step out with Him has given her a great depth of experience, and she constantly sees God's love released through the miraculous. In her first book of poetry, Penelope gives you a glimpse into her personal friendship with the Lord and invites us all to come deeper with Jesus. Her words paint a picture of the goodness of God and Penelope stands in faith with you for your healing in body, soul, and spirit. Thanks for constantly inspiring me, Penelope!

Tristan Conway
Director, School of Faith
Melbourne, Australia

Acknowledgements

Firstly, to Jesus. Thank you for your love, joy, peace, and this fun adventure you're taking my family and I on. Thank you for the restoration and healing I have received from you personally, through your great love. Thank you for the gift of writing and for depositing the words into my heart, then translating them from pen to paper. Holy Spirit, it is through your friendship and because of you that I was able to prophetically formulate the writings throughout this book. I give you all the glory and honour.

To the School of Faith leaders and students across the globe. Through your prophetic declarations, writing awoke from its slumber within me, and I was able to have the courage to write this book. Thank you!

To my parents, Steve and Sandra. Thank you for your love, prayers, and support throughout life. Thank you for giving me space to heal, grow, and succeed. I started as a 'caterpillar' but now I've grown my wings.

To Nur Adil. Thank you for catching the heart and vision of this book with your beautiful illustrations. You brought what I had in my heart and mind alive.

To Anya McKee and the Torn Curtain Publishing team. Thank you for the gift that you are. Thank you for the excellent service you provided, and for going above and beyond to ensure this book is of the best quality. Anya McKee, this journey has been so much fun. You have become a good friend. I look forward to working with you again in the future.

Poetic Remedies is dedicated to my beautiful treasures, my children Zephaniah and Azayliah. I am thankful for the gift of being your mother. I pray this book will be a legacy for you both to dream big. I pray you will know all the days of your lives how valuable and loved you are. May you marinate in God's love throughout your life.

Contents

INTRODUCTION	1
PART ONE: MENTAL AND EMOTIONAL HEALING	3
Kept in the Red	5
Now Walk it Out	6
Good News for my Blues	7
Dancing Through the Deep	8
Chosen	9
My Heart Joins the Choir	10
Tap Dance	11
Treasures	12
Avalanche	13
I am Loved	14
Victorious Duet	16
Something New	17
Set Free	18
Shepherd's Delight	19
Heart Fully Known	20
Lulled in Bliss	22
Love Sweeps	23
Deep Truth Spills In	24
Cheers to New Drills	26
Love Revived	27
River of Life	28
Peace by Piece	29
Cranium Rewired	30
The Antidote	32
Lathered in Lotions	33
Joy: My Permanent Hīkoi	34
Jive with the Hive	36
My Champions Cheer	38
A Mobile Home for You Alone	39
Masterpiece	40
House of Healing	42
Woven Thread	44

A Hallelujah Echo	45
Shalom	46
Tender Heart	48
Pinocchio Has Got to Go	49
The Mighty Path	50
I am Enough	51
Blessed Assurance	52
I am Made New	54
The Light to My Path	56
Renewed Hope	57
Shake the Dust	58
Help is Near	59
Revitalised	60
Rays	61
Insight	62
Kintsugi	63

PART TWO: ENCOUNTERS — **65**

My Rose	67
Sponges	68
The Almighty's Daughter	69
I Belong	70
Sparks in the Making	71
Liquid Love	72
Canopy of Love, Cloud of Peace	74
Look Up	75
Bubbling Brook	76
Liberty	77
My Threads	78
Discovering Treasures	79
A Heartbeat with a Seat	80
Holy Spirit Activate	82
Planted and Granted	84
Decibels of the Almighty	85
Come and Play	86
Heaven's Buff	87
The Door	88
Promises	89
Marinate	90
Direct Mail	91

The Lion's Roar	92
Pivot	93
Open Doors	94
Transports of Delight	95
Beyond the Clock	96
Honey Dew	98
Clothed in Wonder	99
Shouts of Hooray	100
Seated and Celebrated	101
Faithful Companion	102
Living Dust	104
Fresh Spark	105
O, the Song	106
Voice of God	108
Abide	110
Spirit-kissed	112
Awestruck!	113
Fill These Chambers	114
My Faithful One	116
PART THREE: PHYSICAL HEALING	**117**
Autoimmune Diseases Banished	119
Flames of Fire	120
Covid Destroyed	122
Alopecia Evicted	124
Arthritis Expelled	126
Celiac Disease Extracted	128
Diabetes Cured	130
Kidney Disease Flushed	132
Common Cold has no Hold	133
Immune System Rebooted	134
Respiratory System Rewritten	135
A Dance Within Me	136
Chronic Fatigue Zapped	138
Living Without the Pest	140
Life is the Spread	141
Knitted Together	142
The Pop Has Come to a Stop	144
Blossoming Bosom	145
Traded the Pimp	146

Eczema Overthrown	*148*
Obesity Deflated	*150*
Cut Anger, Eat Joy	*151*
Illuminated Crown	*152*
Heart Conditions Retuned	*154*
The Red Thread Remedy	*156*
The Door to Life Swings Wide	*158*
Cancer Eliminated	*160*
Leukaemia Shrivelled	*162*
Metal Liquified	*163*
The Eye of the Rainbow	*164*
Vision Reborn	*165*
Child of Light	*166*
Miracle Shock	*168*
Smells of Victory	*169*
Apple of the Eye	*170*
Macula, You are Spectacular	*172*
Untied	*174*
— Lip Tie Testimony	*175*
Extend Your Tether	*176*
Tongue, Be Loosed	*177*
Cognition Reawakened	*178*
Dyslexia Expelled	*179*
This Noggin Lacks Nothing	*180*
Happy Feet	*183*
Beautiful Ears	*184*
Ditch the High Pitch	*186*
Long Live These Bones	*188*
New Story	*190*
Miracle Gear	*192*
Love is in the Air	*195*
Remarkably Cured	*196*
Balanced	*198*
— Leg Lengthened Testimony	*199*
GETTING TO KNOW JESUS	**201**
AUTHOR'S NOTE	**203**
FINAL WORDS	**205**
ABOUT THE AUTHOR	**207**

Introduction

Dear friend, I am so thrilled this book is in your hands. *Poetic Remedies* is a collection of poems written by inspiration of the Holy Spirit. May love, joy and peace flood your whole being as you marinate in the goodness of God spilled on these pages in both the written and the unwritten lines. Words can be life giving or poisonous. May these words become like healing morsels for every inch of you, from the top of your head to the soles of your feet.

As you read, I invite you to position your heart to receive. Humility is essential as we apply the healing balm. You only need to believe healing is for you and receive it as yours. Hope will begin to pop up in your life like a beautiful garden.

I have included several testimonies in the final section of this book. A testimony is a story that displays the goodness of God in someone's life. It is evidence of God's love for us. Acts 10:34 says: "Now I know for certain that God doesn't show favouritism with people but treats everyone on the same basis" (TPT). This means that what God does for one person He can do for you! By sharing testimonies, we are saying, "Do it again!" May these testimonies encourage you and increase your faith and hope for what is possible in your own life.

In Revelation 19:10, John wrote:

> *I am a fellow servant with you and your brothers and sisters who have and hold the testimony of Jesus. Worship God [alone]. For the testimony of Jesus is the spirit of prophecy [His life and teaching are the heart of prophecy]. (AMP)*

These poetic remedies are prophetic. What do I mean by prophetic? Prophecy is calling into being things that don't exist yet (Romans 4:17). When applying these 'remedies', read them aloud as a declaration. You could even read them over yourself three times a day, just as you might take medicine prescribed by your doctor three times daily!

You will notice I have chosen to address you, the reader, using the word, "We". This is because as I speak, I am intentionally positioning myself alongside the Trinity—Father, Son and Holy Spirit. Together we delight in you and declare healing over every aspect of your life—your mind, emotions, spirit and body.

Everyone who came to Jesus was healed. I believe that He is good, and He desires to heal you because He loves you. You don't need to perform your way into healing. You are his delight; you are his 'good thoughts'. By his wounds we are healed (Isaiah 53:5). So come like a child and receive your free gift. Healing can be instant, or it can happen gradually over time. Either way, it's miraculous! Keep thanking Jesus for your healing. As you read aloud and declare these poems and scriptures over yourself, or a loved one, continue to believe for your miracle! I champion you as you choose to step into the journey of wholeness.

Before you read further, I would like to pray for you:

Together with Holy Spirit, I release healing and creative miracles over you. I loose and release joy and peace over your body from the top of your head to the soles of your feet. May your life be transformed by radical encounters with God that draw you closer and deeper in relationship with him. Jesus, pour out your love on this precious reader. Make their heart brand new. Restore their mind and heal their memories. Let them tangibly experience your love right now. Jesus, would you dispatch your angels to shield, protect and bless their life? Thank you for what you have done, will do, and are about to do for this precious reader. In the mighty name of Jesus, Amen.

Part One

MENTAL AND EMOTIONAL HEALING

To the one who is searching for love. There is a love so deep it heals and hugs you inside, causing your very organs to dance.

Kept in the Red

Love spoke
Love awoke
Love chose
Love spilled
Love arose

God is love
I am loved

Love flows
Love fills
Love speaks
Love gives
Love heals
Love restores
Love creates
Love has no end

God is love
I am kept in your love

God is love, and he who abides in love abides in God, and God in him. 1 John 4:16 NKJV

For further declaration: John 15:13 | Romans 5:5 | 1 John 4:10

Are you needing a boost in faith to believe for healing, prosperity, or breakthrough in whatever promise you have in your heart from the Lord?

Now Walk it Out

From thought, to speech, to existence
Miracles at the tip of your tongue
Transition into receiving

Walk as though it's already done
Celebrate the gift that was hung
For love has risen
And keeps on giving

For all of God's promises have been fulfilled in Christ with a resounding "Yes!" And through Christ, our "Amen" (which means "Yes") ascends to God for his glory. 2 Corinthians 1:20

For further declaration: Isaiah 55:11 | Psalm 100:4 | John 16:24

To the one who is feeling the weight of life's pressures. The mental and emotional pain of the sorrows you carry are weighing you down. We encourage you to stop replaying this narrative in your mind and exchange it for good news. Let go, healing is on your doorstep! Allow the love of Jesus to sweep through those tough spaces in your life. As you lay or sit in his presence, invite him to sing songs that will transport you to a place, where the blues become out of place. Joy is chasing after you today.

Good News for my Blues

Laying still in your presence
The warmth of your gaze on my face
You sing over my blues with good news
It's you that I choose

Here's the one thing I crave from Yahweh, the one thing I seek above all else: I want to live with him every moment in his house, beholding the marvelous beauty of Yahweh, filled with awe, delighting in his glory and grace. I want to contemplate in his temple. Psalm 27:4 TPT

For further declaration: Zephaniah 3:17 | Psalm 16:11 | Psalm 30:11 | Psalm 126:5

To the ones who keep to themselves because of past hurts, not knowing who to trust. You were born to be a flowing river, not a reservoir. We invite you to begin dancing through the deep waters, allowing your heart to be washed from wounds and hurts. As you do, your heart will begin to flow with new songs. Come out from the shadows that cast you into loneliness. We release hope, courage and love. Allow your heart to awaken from its slumber and anchor into hope once again. Receive the deposit of love, never looking back.

Dancing Through the Deep

These streams started as tears
But you stirred the waters
Creating rivers that flow
Not a reservoir that keeps to oneself

You call me your own
I'm never going back
Flowing forward
These currents breathe life

Dancing through deep waters
Your songs of joy bring my heart to life
You deposit your love inside

You are the waterfall
Changing what was bad to good
The fresh flow where hope stood

When you go through deep waters, I will be with you. When you go through rivers of difficulty, you will not drown. Isaiah 43:2

For further declaration: Psalm 56:8 | Romans 8:28 | Ephesians 2:10 | John 7:38

To the one who needs to be reminded that your life matters and you are here with a purpose. It doesn't matter what you have or haven't done. You are enough, and you are chosen. You are the one Jesus longs to spend time with. There is nothing you can do that will make him love you more—or less. You are a treasure, a beautiful fragrant flower. Amongst all the people in the world, Jesus has chosen you! We release joy over you and say to insight, "switch on," so that you will know deeply that you are wanted, and you are loved.

Chosen

Amongst all the flowers
I choose you everyday

Your smile shines bright
Like a healthy dose of sunlight

You didn't choose me. I chose you. John 15:16

Yes, you are my darling companion. You stand out from all the rest. For though the thorns surround you, you remain as pure as a lily, more than all the others. Song of Songs 2:2 TPT

For further declaration: Lamentations 3:22-23 | 1 Peter 2:9 | Psalm 139

To the one who is feeling discouraged. Hope has been deferred, and disappointment has silenced your voice. Maybe you have found yourself sitting in comparison. You don't know how you got here, but you are in a state where you can't see what's good around you—like someone has turned the lights off. We invite you to look at Jesus. He is good. He is turning the lights back on. Allow him to give you a fresh perspective. The things you are hoping and longing for will come through. Join in with creation who are already praising. There are trees dancing, flowers kissing you with fragrance, and wind wrapping around you like an invisible hug. As your heart joins in with the choir, the praise will wash over your disappointment and shift you back to hope. We must not let our problems become bigger than our God. Allow these words to breathe new wind into your sail. Bring to your memory the good things he has done. We release angels to surround you with songs of triumph.

My Heart Joins the Choir

Waves, you are calling me
Crash over me!
Wind, a burst
of your energy
Your mercy is tender
Hallelujah

Trees, dance
Birds, sing
What a mighty King!
My heart longs for you
more than anything

For your steadfast love is before my eyes, and I walk in your faithfulness. Psalm 26:3 ESV

For further declaration: Psalm 84 | Isaiah 55:12 | Psalm 29:9 | Psalm 96 | Psalm 63:2-4

Have you closed off your heart? The emotional pain lingers like a bad smell. You may feel like you don't know which way is up. You may feel unseen, unworthy, uninvited, or unlovable. Surrender your heart today. Jesus the Messiah is a loving God who kisses away the hurts, chases down the lies you believe about yourself, and sweeps you into a dance—a dance of love lavishing inside you, nourishing every organ within you. Like raindrops dancing across the window, allow these words to wash over your heart and mind. Can you hear that gentle tapping? Today this dance ushers you into colours of promise.

Tap Dance

As the rain falls, I lavish nourishment into you
Tap dancing on the window with every rain drop
Colours of promise
Tones of gentleness

Howling in the wind
The sound of a fierce pursuit
Calling me deeper
Chasing me down

I am caught up and found
Where your beauty abounds

Your beauty and love chase after me every day of my life. Psalm 23:6 MSG

Deep calls unto deep at the noise of Your waterfalls; all Your waves and billows have gone over me. The Lord will command His lovingkindness in the daytime, and in the night His song shall be with me. Psalm 42:7-8 NKJV

For further declaration: 1 John 3:1 | Psalm 90:17 | Psalm 17:8 | 1 John 4:19

Do you feel like life has slipped from your fingers? You cannot see ahead, and when you look back it's crowded with regret and loss. Maybe you find yourself longing to step onto the abundant path of life, leaving poverty in the rear view along with the smoke and dust. No matter how young or old you are, we crush all obstacles holding you back from getting ahead. We unhook regret and loss from its vacuum. We speak repairs into the greedy holes you were left with. We awaken identity and purpose within you. We release treasures into your life today. We release joy as a mark of your life, a companion to help you amongst the grit in your journey. Dive past the circumference! There is so much you cannot see at this moment, but your path is bright. Today, may you have the sense of knowing you are holding treasures.

Treasures

I'm never late to set the plate
What's awake will start to quake
Rest in the intake of what I bake
All obstacles are crushed like a snake

Treasures are unfolding
Wisdom is sewing
Vision is growing
Knowledge is brewing
In the wind I am wooing

May this journey be witty amongst the gritty
Pouring joy on the kitty litter
Paths of abundance
Diving past the circumference

Look, I have given you authority over all the power of the enemy, and you can walk among snakes and scorpions and crush them. Nothing will injure you. Luke 10:19

For further declaration: Psalm 31:19 | Proverbs 3:13-18 | Psalm 36:8 | Philippians 4:19

To the one whose life has taken many twists and turns and you're wondering when you will catch a break from this wild storm. We release a change in perspective today. God is breathing his abundant blessings on you. We release an avalanche of joy. Catch the wave of blessings upon blessings.

Avalanche

Rolling quickly to the new
An open door to your arms
Love engulfs my lungs
I see a dam bursting
Joyful waters flowing

The current is your heartbeat
Singing exuberant songs
Yahweh! Lacking nothing!

Water colours the painting
Night and day you stroke on the story—and the song
Yahweh, Yahweh, Yahweh—the inhale, and the exhale
Life, breath of abundance
You are my avalanche

Things are going to happen so fast your head will swim, one thing fast on the heels of the other. You won't be able to keep up. Everything will be happening at once—and everywhere you look, blessings! Blessings like wine pouring off the mountains and hills. Amos 9:13 MSG

For further declaration: Genesis 2:7 | Job 32:8 | Jeremiah 29:11

Do you feel left out or forgotten? You may feel you have lost your sense of worth because life's circumstances have robbed you of your identity. We release the truth of who you really are. You are loved, yes! You are loved. God is love, and he loves you with an everlasting love. We release redemption from what was robbed from you. We speak innocence and purity over your entire being. Discover your identity from the safety of the arms of your Creator. It is an explosive joy dance between you and the Trinity that unlocks the real you.

———

I am Loved

Today is the day I celebrate you
Every day my love is everlasting towards you
I keep you close, I am in your every breath
I am yours and you are mine
I whisper my ways to help guide you

Every branch of my vine
brings strength and new wine

This is a new year
Wisdom and understanding
Will flow from the depths of you
You release light to those around you
Life-changing results
Releasing captives on catapults
Prisoners from their vaults

Keep drawing near to me
As we sing this sweet melody
You are my bright, shining delight
I am with you even when things seem out of sight

Receive my waves of love,
My peace covering you from above
I am the hand, you are my glove
We move as one, my beautiful one

All through the day Yahweh has commanded his endless love to pour over me. Through the night I sing his songs and my praises to the living God. Psalm 42:8 TPT

Where could I go from your Spirit? Where could I run and hide from your face? If I go down to the realm of the dead, you're there too! If I fly with wings into the shining dawn, you're there! If I fly into the radiant sunset, you're there waiting! Wherever I go, your hand will guide me; your strength will empower me. Psalm 139:7-10 TPT

For further declaration: John 3:16 | Zephaniah 3:17 | Jeremiah 31:3

To the one who is carrying stress from the many cares that are piling up around you. Your mind may feel distracted, and you may feel distant with all that is going on. Fear has started to rise, but you want to jump out of that suffocating trap. We encourage you to let go of your cares and place them in your loving King's hands. Allow him to bathe you in his goodness and mercy. Join in with his song, a timely duet. Victory is already yours.

Victorious Duet

Laid my heart bare
With every care
Head to toe
Soaking in your goodness
Cocooned in your kindness
Your everlasting love kissing away
The hurts, the stresses,
And all the fuss the heart conducts—when it gets distracted

Gazing at the stars of many
Your love stretches further
My magnificent One
Preparing day break with new songs to be sung
You calm the storm of wiggling organs
You sweep me back into the chorus
Our duet dancing on the mountain peak

Victory is ours
Thank you for silencing the howls

The God of passionate love will meet with me. My God will empower me to rise in triumph over my foes. Psalm 59:10 TPT

For further declaration: Psalm 98 | Ephesians 5:19 | Psalm 55:22 | 1 Peter 5:7

To the one whose soul is feeding on ugly lies. Maybe you were verbally and emotionally abused. You feel you are in the thick of it; pain is pinning you down and you can't stand another shred of it. We want you to know that the broken places you have faced do not define you. There is nothing so big that it cannot be healed, renewed and restored. Come out of the grave of destruction—it is not where you belong. A canopy of goodness is within reach. Allow these words to drip like honey, bringing life to your very being. We cut off the weight you have been living under and release a tangible scent of honey for you to inhale. There is something new for you today.

Something New

The canopy of your goodness
Soothes the aches within
The weight disappears

I see you shoot up a flare
As I trade and stand bare
You are near, whispering truth for every care
The air has become light to breathe
The scent of honey travels down the nasal path
I'm sinking into something new (Breathe in deeply)

Escort me into your truth; take me by the hand and teach me. For you are the God of my salvation; I have wrapped my heart into yours all day long! Psalm 25:5 TPT

Pleasant words are like a honeycomb, sweet and delightful to the soul and healing to the body. Proverbs 16:24 AMP

For further declaration: Psalm 119:103 | Proverbs 16:24 | Matthew 11:28-30

To the one who has been living with sickness or disease. You may have asked for healing many times but haven't received it yet. Pivot to praise today! Praise focuses your eyes on the solution, not the problem. We encourage you to fight your battles with praise. You don't need to see it or feel it to believe it. Healing is yours, and in God's presence there is fullness of joy. A cheerful heart is good medicine, so let's start with the good medicine for your soul. Praising God whether things are going well or things feel crummy is important. Catch a glimpse of heaven on earth; leave no room for your hope to defer. God is good, and he wants you free. We release peace over your thoughts and emotions. We release an increase of faith to keep on believing and asking. We praise alongside you. We release joy into the DNA of your being. May you be flooded with light.

Set Free

His stripes have set me free
I'm swimming in streams with glee
You are singing over me
Oh, just look at your majesty!

But He was wounded for our transgressions, He was crushed for our wickedness [our sin, our injustice, our wrongdoing]; The punishment [required] for our well-being fell on Him, and by His stripes (wounds) we are healed. Isaiah 53:5 AMP

The Lord your God is in your midst, a mighty one who will save; he will rejoice over you with gladness; he will quiet you by his love; he will exult over you with loud singing. Zephaniah 3:17 ESV

For further declaration: 1 Chronicles 16:27 | Psalm 145:5

To the one who feels discarded, of no value, lost, or forgotten. Perhaps you have been searching for something to fill the gap in your heart. The Lord does not make mistakes. He delights in you. It is through a relationship with Jesus that you discover who you are, because as He is, so are you. We release overwhelming love and joy. We release life and light, pulling back the curtains that have kept you isolated. You are written on the palm of his hand. We release identity. You are significant. May you sense God's pleasure in you. We speak an awakening of your true worth. The Good Shepherd has found you today. Allow him to wrap around you like a shield.

Shepherd's Delight

Blinds rolled back
Basked in light
Dark hole filled
Shepherd-led

I am found
Flooded with love
Expansive light
Shepherd's delight

The Lord takes pleasure in all he has made! Psalm 104:31

The Son of Man has come to give life to all who are lost. Think of it this way: If a man owns a hundred sheep and one lamb wanders away and is lost, won't he leave the ninety-nine grazing the hillside and thoroughly search for the one lost lamb? And if he finds his lost lamb, he rejoices over it, more than over the ninety-nine that never went astray. Now you should understand that it is never the desire of your heavenly Father that a single one of these little ones should be lost. Matthew 18:12-14 TPT

For further declaration: Romans 5:5 | James 1:17 | John 10:27 | Psalm 97:11

To the one who feels anonymous, who has blocked off their heart so people cannot get close. Trusting again seems impossible, but you desire to be known. You long to receive love and to love once again in return. We release courage! Allow your heart to flow in the beauty of love again. Your Creator designed you to love and be loved. We release contagious joy and deep belly laughter. It's beginning to bubble up now—can you feel it? We release a fresh wind to untangle the knots that strangle any connection that is good. We invite you to drink of a love that never runs dry. A love poured out like balm, healing shattered hearts. A love that works things together for good. A love that always draws near. A love that whispers day and night how valuable and treasured you are. A love that provides and promotes. A love that restores and redeems your past. A love that connects the right people to your path. A love that was whipped, spat on, and hung on a cross just so you could have a relationship with him. A love that purchased your freedom, healing and salvation. A love that knew you before you were even born and has good thoughts towards you, giving you a hope and a future. Marinate in this love. From this place of total saturation, allow the Holy Spirit to lead you until it flows to those around you.

Heart Fully Known

In a moment
Time stood still
I heard the symphony my heart was thumping

Off tune

Something blocking the flow of red
In the depths of what seemed like a grave
A choice was made

Unclogged

There's a fountain flowing
A heart that's known

Fully known

Safe in this place

My cup running over
Splashes on the pavement

From love received
Love is freely given
To each one that comes in vision
I drink from the red
In which my heart is found

Lord, you know everything there is to know about me. You perceive every movement of my heart and soul, and you understand my every thought before it even enters my mind. You are so intimately aware of me, Lord. You read my heart like an open book and you know all the words I'm about to speak before I even start a sentence! You know every step I will take before my journey even begins. Psalm 139:1-4 TPT

You feed them from the abundance of your own house, letting them drink from your river of delights. Psalm 36:8

For further declaration: Proverbs 4:23 | John 15:12 | Psalm 126:5 | Romans 5:5

To the one who has a heart full of envy, wanting all the things other people have. This has left you unsatisfied, and gratitude has gone out of view. Carrying heaviness in your heart is not a pleasant way to live. Trade these ill findings with rest and peace. We break off the choking hold that comparison has left you in. Turn from the rottenness of envy. Run to your Creator who will never leave you in lack. We release harmony and tranquillity over your heart. Choose to celebrate others and allow the Holy Spirit to unpack your unique story.

Lulled in Bliss

I am lulled in bliss
My body submerged in harmony
My eyes gazing upon you
My heart becomes tranquil
I choose rest
You meet me here

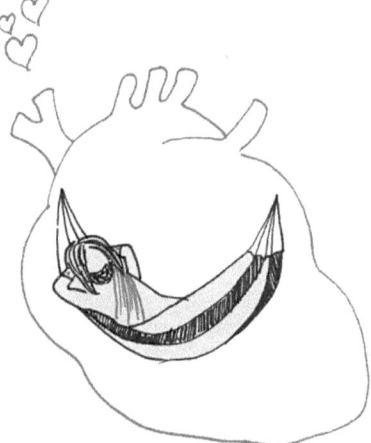

He offers a resting place for me in his luxurious love. His tracks take me to an oasis of peace near the quiet brook of bliss. Psalm 23:2 TPT

A calm, peaceful, and tranquil heart is life and health to the body, but passion and envy are like rottenness to the bones. Proverbs 14:30 AMP

For further declaration: Matthew 5:8 | Matthew 11:28-29 | Zephaniah 3:17

To the one who has been avoiding pain. Grief has been piling up. We encourage you to feel that pain and allow it to propel you into your healing. What happened to you was bitter and sour. Today Jesus wants the sweetness of his love to fill those spaces. Acknowledging the pain is the first step. As you cross the bridge you will be greeted with strength. The joy of the Lord is your strength. Can you hear the knocking at the door of your heart? Jesus is inviting you to feast with him. We release restoration over the years of heartache, sorrow, loss, and destruction. We release generational blessings. We bless your heart with love that sweeps you into wholeness. There is a joyful dance taking place. When you spin around, take notice that goodness and mercy are following your every step.

Love Sweeps

A bridge
From past to present
Broken by fears and cares
—Not beyond repair

Feel the sting
Acknowledge the ring
Goodness is weaving
Joyful songs sinking
Into the skin

As you cross the bridge
Dust becomes robust
Love sweeps
Trust greets

For the Lord is good. His unfailing love continues forever, and his faithfulness continues to each generation. Psalm 100:5

For further declaration: Isaiah 40:31 | 1 John 4:4 | Revelation 3:20 | 2 Corinthians 5:17

To the one who has been harbouring unforgiveness. You expected it to punish the other person, but it has actually left you in torment. We release love that washes over your pain, guilt or shame. We break off the offense that hijacked your joy and peace. We speak healing over the negative thoughts that have been playing on repeat. We release strength and courage to choose forgiveness. We release freedom. We invite wisdom and understanding to help you to intentionally reject the hook of offense and extend forgiveness even if it hurts. Living in forgiveness blesses the generations coming after you. Plant the best seeds for your loved ones. May blessings flow and truth spill deeply into your heart today.

Deep Truth Spills In

Surrendered
Forgiven
Uncaged from prison
Poison extracted
Thoughts evicted
Unremitting clips expunged
Love invited
Deep truth spills in

Identity strengthened
Wrongs no longer collected
Offense not accepted
Seventy times seven extended

Cleansed in you
Mind renewed
Blessings enlarged
Predetermined forgiveness
No more wrongs for a witness
Torment is snuffed
Kept in your love

Those who live to bless others will have blessings heaped upon them, and the one who pours out his life to pour out blessings will be saturated with favor. Proverbs 11:25 TPT

But you, dear friends, must build each other up in your most holy faith, pray in the power of the Holy Spirit, and await the mercy of our Lord Jesus Christ, who will bring you eternal life. In this way, you will keep yourselves safe in God's love. Jude 1:20-21

For further declaration: 1 Corinthians 13:4 | John 8:32

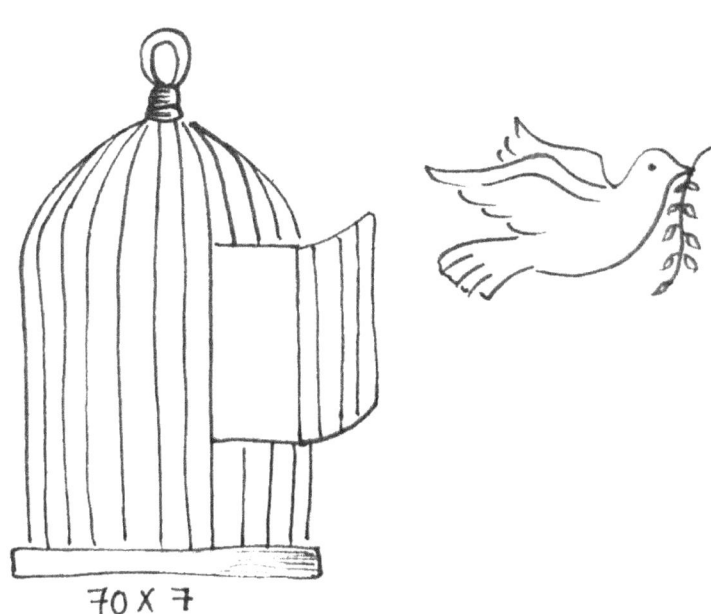

70 X 7

To the one who is looking for new beginnings and renewed hope. Winter can feel cold, barren, desolate, and we can grow discouraged. But if we imagine all that is happening underground, waiting for spring to emerge, we can have hope. God is always at work, even when we can't see or feel it. Similarly, our lives have seasons. In our pain we can end up switching our love off. Love going cold only isolates us. Remember, not every thought that enters your mind is your own. What you choose to think and dwell on affects your quality of life. We release the ability to discern the thoughts you should pay attention to and the thoughts that are destined for the rubbish bin. Today we light the candle in your heart once again. Pain is melting away and vision is being painted before you. The baton you hold will pass to the generations behind you. Cheers to new drills!

Cheers to New Drills

Catch the wave
Walk out the grave
Darts ricochet
Death gets no say
Life makes no room for it to stay

Winter around my heart
Is melted by your art
You breathe a fresh new start

I'm choosing the green hill
Vision thrills
Love fills
Hope spills
Cheers to new drills.

God, the Lord, is my strength; he makes my feet like the deer's; he makes me tread on my high places. Habakkuk 3:19 ESV

For further declaration: Isaiah 54:17 | Ephesians 6:16 | Luke 24:32 | Song of Songs 2:10-11

Are you going through heartbreak? Things may seem dim at the moment, but this ends today. Jesus wants to bring colour back into your life. He is near to the broken-hearted. God not only loves you—his very essence is love. Allow him to put you back together and revive you.

Love Revived

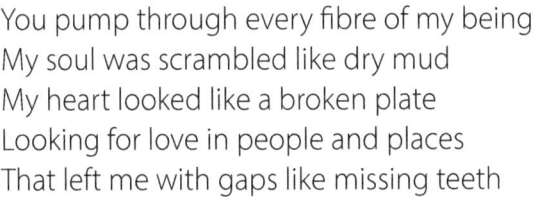

These veins celebrate!
I choose you but you chose me first
Your love poured out
Has taken this body out of drought

You pump through every fibre of my being
My soul was scrambled like dry mud
My heart looked like a broken plate
Looking for love in people and places
That left me with gaps like missing teeth

I was uninvited but finally I saw the invitation you give daily
In the distort you caught every tear that was shed
In the dim of black and white
Colour came into view
Love was always standing in front of me!

You are love
Liquid love
Fiery love
Everlasting love

This hope will not lead us to disappointment. For we know how dearly God loves us, because he has given us the Holy Spirit to fill our hearts with love. Romans 5:5

For further declaration: Isaiah 57:14-15, 18-19 | Psalm 34:18 | Luke 1:37 | Revelation 3:20

Trade your frustrations for wisdom and understanding. You are set apart for victory my friend. Submerge in the river of life where Jesus restores your health and dips you in wisdom. May you be like salmon swimming upstream, drawing close to Jesus. It is in him you live, move, and have your being.

River of Life

O breath, O wind, you envelop me
–and bathe me in the depths of peace
Ruach HaKodesh, my faithful companion
Today I let go of all my frustrations
I call forth wisdom and understanding
I lay bare this dirty air
Stepping in, submerging myself
Into the rivers of your wealth
You restore my health

As I listen within, I hear bubbles thickening
My faith in you is beckoning
I am in you
You are in me
In you I live, move, and have my being

My God has set me apart for victory!
Day and night
Things keep looking bright
As I choose to trust
–and thank you
I declare your praises, you keep me in your wonderful light

You feed them from the abundance of your own house, letting them drink from your river of delights. Psalm 36:8

For further declaration: Proverbs 2:2-5 | Romans 10:17 | Proverbs 3:5-8 | John 14:26

Does fear grip you? Do you want to be free? Allow Jesus' love to wash over you. Fear has run out of breath. Come to the table and feed on his truth. Pay attention to the peace that enters your heart and mind as you feast.

Peace by Piece

Fear, when you stare
You will listen to the music I blare
All you get to see is my rear

Fear, you may peer
But these lips sear

Fear, you are garbage rotting in the air
Hissing thoughts to despair

Fear, you used to wear and tear
Whoops, where's your hair?

Fear, you've become bald
No growth for you to hold

Fear, you are like a brown apple
Exposed
Door closed

Fear, your lies have gone—Bye-bye
You won't catch my breath
Fear, I've crossed over to peace
It has become my feast
Night and day
Peace by piece

You will keep in perfect peace all who trust in you, Isaiah 26:3

For further declaration: Psalm 94:19, 34:4 | Philippians 4:6-9 | Joshua 1:8 | John 14:27

To the one who struggles or has issues with mental health—it could be autism spectrum disorder (ASD), depression, or anxiety. Read the words in this poem that apply to you. Allow your mind and heart to experience peace as these words wash over you. I bless you with joy. Be filled with the Holy Spirit. You are made whole!

Cranium Rewired

Mental health,
Your shelves are out of order and bursting full
I sever your origins of destruction and pull out your roots
Be realigned like a dotted "i" and crossed "t"
39 stripes and a cross-shaped tree has set you free

Autism Spectrum Disorder,
Your temporal cortex has thickened up
like frosting laid on a cake
Your enlarged amygdalae is now resized like the perfect jewel placed on your finger
Your entire cerebrum has been rewired
Dispatch red flames of fire
Lithium and strontium sulphate, create and recreate
I am made whole

Depression,
The material you were served was coded in darkness
I assign you a new comprehension
You are now flooded with light
Joy has magnetised to you
Dispatch red flames of fire
Lithium and strontium sulphate, create and recreate
I am made whole

Anxiety,
You have left me sick with apprehension
Your distress has been too excessive
You have been scrapped off like burnt toast
I see liberty
Surges of love pulsate through me
Dispatch red flames of fire
Lithium and strontium sulphate, create and recreate
I am made whole

For I know the thoughts that I think toward you, says the Lord, thoughts of peace and not of evil, to give you a future and a hope. Jeremiah 29:11 NKJV

He is so rich in kindness and grace that he purchased our freedom with the blood of his Son and forgave our sins. He has showered his kindness on us, along with all wisdom and understanding. Ephesians 1:7-8

For further declaration: Mark 5:2-15 | 2 Corinthians 3:17 | Acts 8:7-8

Jesus is the antidote to your big emotions. We release giggles that wiggle within you, bringing your heart back to bliss. You are a precious treasure. Allow Jesus to dote on you until he becomes your antidote that flows in all your life.

The Antidote

>Whiffs of the rose
>The channel I chose
>Giggles that flow
>The antidote you know

A joyful, cheerful heart brings healing to both body and soul. Proverbs 17:22 TPT

For further declaration: 2 Corinthians 2:15

Do you have confusion or noisy disturbance in your life? We set you free from that today. We release peace and clarity over your situations and circumstances. Allow Jesus to fine-tune your emotions and take you deeper in his devotion to you. Jesus is lathering you in his great love.

Lathered in Lotions

A spring in motion
Stems from your devotion
You lather me in your lotions
Fine tuning my emotions

Something has awoken
Your words like honey
–as you've spoken
You dust off the broken
Cut off the commotion
Reset and bring promotion
Lead me back to the ocean

May you have the power to understand, as all God's people should, how wide, how long, how high, and how deep his love is. May you experience the love of Christ, though it is too great to understand fully. Then you will be made complete with all the fullness of life and power that comes from God. Ephesians 3:18-19

For further declaration: Psalm 30:11 | Psalm 119:25 | Romans 10:17

Do you want to live a life full of joy? Joy is one of the nine attributes of a person living in accord with the Holy Spirit. Joy doesn't depend on what's happening, what you have, who's in your life—or not in your life. Joy is a choice, an attitude of the heart determined by confidence in God. Joy doesn't mean forcing happiness during sad circumstances. Joy is an outpouring of the Holy Spirit. Joy strengthens you; it brings life to your body and makes your bones glow. Joy heals, refreshes, shifts toxic atmospheres, and flows like a river within you. It is constant, it inspires creativity, and sometimes it comes as a deep belly-laugh. A merry heart is good medicine. Allow joy to sit on your face. It's hovering like a helicopter, waiting to land. We invite you to choose joy as your permanent hīkoi (Māori word for 'walk').

Joy: My Permanent Hīkoi

Your living grace lingering as I see you face to face
The sounds of the mouth come forth
Unknown language designed by you
Dancing music
Spirit to spirit
Shifting the pong when something is wrong
Calling on wisdom when insight is out of rhythm
Releasing shalom, suffocating fear till it's gone
Inviting joy as my permanent hīkoi

Bathing in your goodness
Truth rushing in as a witness
Transformation from every direction
Creative explosion
A confidence boost and a light on the post
A deep knowing of your love that is flowing
Connection brewing in all that you're sowing
Hidden secrets spoken into existence
Plenty of reasons to praise your mighty name

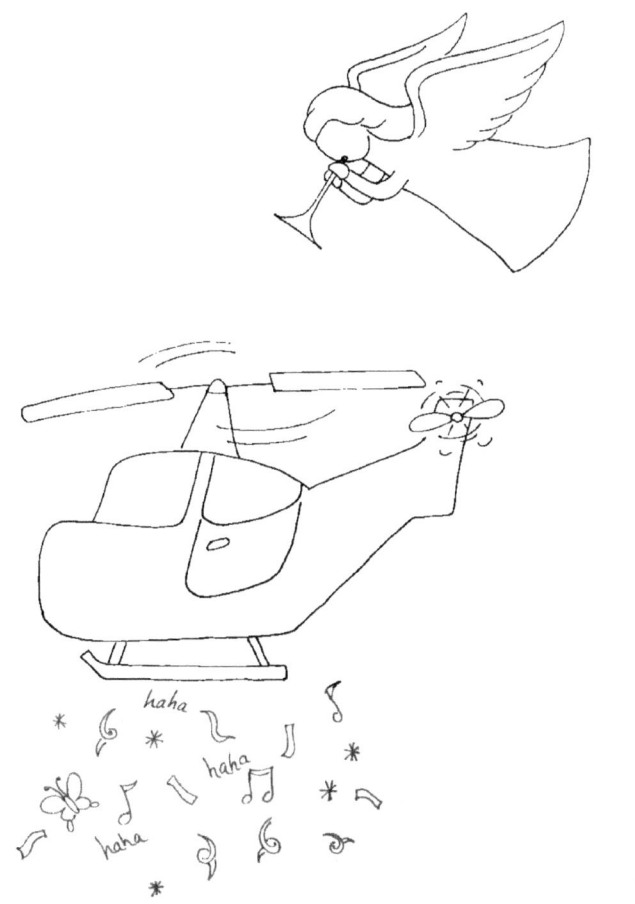

Let joy be your continual feast. 1 Thessalonians 5:16 TPT

If you wait at wisdom's doorway, longing to hear a word for every day, joy will break forth within you as you listen for what I'll say. For the fountain of life pours into you every time that you find me, and this is the secret of growing in the delight and the favor of the Lord. Proverbs 8:34 TPT

For further declaration: Proverbs 4:5-8 | Proverbs 4:21-22 | John 16:13-14 | Isaiah 26:3

Do you have dreams that seem lost or dead? Maybe you are mourning a loved one. Disappointment shatters your heart. We move you out of this state and into joy and love everlasting. When you have no words to express what's going on within you, begin to sing in tongues. The Holy Spirit helps you in your weakness with groanings that cannot be expressed in words. The Lord is already in your midst, singing over you. Can you hear him singing? His words dissipate the heaviness and burdens that have been sitting deep in your heart. His words are like honey, they nourish your very soul. You can find shelter in the love of Jesus. His angels have been sent to cover and protect you. No weapon formed against you shall prosper. Allow Jesus to breathe life into your circumstances. Just as Jesus called out Lazarus from the tomb, you can start calling out your dreams. May your heart be filled afresh with love. Begin to jive with the hive.

Jive with the Hive

There are wings for every sting
When you sing things go ping!
You'll find a jive with every hive
May every cell come alive
(Fill in the blank) _____, come out!

He will cover you with his feathers, He will shelter you with his wings. His faithful promises are your armor and protection. Psalm 91:4

For further declaration: Ezekiel 37:4-10 | Isaiah 54:17 | Hebrews 4:12 | John 11:43-44

Do you feel like a failure? Are you carrying burdens? Jesus has paid for your freedom. He will sustain and uphold you. He watches over you day and night. He is cheering you on. Can you hear him cheer? Glean from his words that are sweet like honey. Be reminded of his delight in you.

My Champions Cheer

Can you hear the cheer?
Well done, faithful one
You are seen
You are clean
I am pleased with you

Leaning in . . .

Yes, I can hear your mighty cheer
I see performance disappear
It doesn't matter where I've been
It doesn't matter what I do

Just being me is enough
I am seen
I am clean
It is your cheer that I hear

For he enjoys his faithful lovers. He adorns the humble with his beauty, and he loves to give them victory. Psalm 149:4 TPT

For further declaration: Psalm 55:22 | Psalm 34:15 | Psalm 34:22 | Matthew 3:17

Jesus sees your pain. He is reaching out and touching your heart today. He is infusing you with his love, his supernatural fire. In your pain you can praise the Lord in ways you can't when things are going well. There is no space for pain to reside in your heart when you come to Jesus to heal you. Today your pain is being replaced with joy and hope. Your heart has become a hearth. Will you allow your heart to burn for him alone? When your heart burns for Jesus it brings hope; others jump around the campfire and receive his love too. Your life is bigger than your own. Do you know the power that resides within you? The same Spirit that raised Jesus from the dead lives within you. Things happen around you and to you that Jesus wants to partner with you to change. Will you partner with him? Choose to commune with God at all times, no matter how you feel. As you get to know him more you will see that as he is, so are you. Wherever you go, he is ready to shift atmospheres around you and speak through you.

A Mobile Home for You Alone

Your hand reached out
Lit a match from your heart
Leaned in to impart
I am infused with fire
I have become a hearth
A mobile home for you alone

Have you forgotten that your body is now the sacred temple of the Spirit of Holiness, who lives in you? You don't belong to yourself any longer, for the gift of God, the Holy Spirit, lives inside your sanctuary. 1 Corinthians 6:19 TPT

For further declaration: Psalm 39:3 | Jeremiah 23:29 | Hebrews 12:29

Do you have doubts about who you are? When God created you, he did so in the image of himself. You are his good thoughts. You are fearfully and wonderfully made. Invite Jesus to speak to you about who you truly are. God doesn't make mistakes. You are a masterpiece. He has set you apart for great things. Your life was written out before you were even born. The world is waiting for you to add salt to the earth—a flavour that can only be expressed through you and your relationship with Jesus.

Masterpiece

My life is a poem
I am art set apart!

I am chosen, holy and blameless
I am a branch of the true vine
I am a fellow heir with Christ
I am a new creature

I am the righteousness of God in Christ
I am seated in heavenly places with Christ
I am a citizen of heaven

I am creative
I am loved
I am God's delight
I am salt and light

I have been redeemed and forgiven
I have been sealed with the Holy Spirit of promise
I have boldness and confidently access God through faith in Christ

Every spiritual blessing is mine
The peace of God guards my heart and mind
God supplies all my needs

My life is a poem
I am art set apart!

My creator designed me
No-one else can define me
I am a masterpiece

For we are God's masterpiece. Ephesians 2:10

We have become his poetry. Ephesians 2:10 TPT

For further declaration: Genesis 1:26 | Ephesians 1:4 | Psalm 139

Do you know that you are a house of healing? You might have sickness in your body—that is a fact. But the truth is, you carry within you the same Spirit that raised Jesus from the dead. That resurrection life brings healing, miracles and joy to your mind, body, soul and spirit. Jesus doesn't just heal; He is healer. As he is, so are you. Begin to live out the truth that you are a house of healing. What you think about grows. Picture yourself well and healthy. Choose to dwell on the goodness of God and expect it to overflow in your life. Faith comes by hearing, and hearing by the word of God. Begin to declare who you are. Your body will respond to the truth. You create with your mouth. While you are waiting for your healing to be evidenced in your body, do not change your confession. Just keep thanking him. Your words are life or death. Which will you speak?

House of Healing

I am a house of healing
I am a castle of joy
I am a mansion of miracles
I am a castle of joy

'Cause as you are, so am I
As you are, so am I

May this house hear conversations
–filled with celebration
There are no limits to this house
Your love holds me together
Faith is my doors and windows

I am a house of healing
I am a mansion of miracles
I am a castle of joy

The Spirit of the living God lives within me
And me and my house serve the Lord

O Lord, my healing God, I cried out for a miracle and you healed me! Psalm 30:2 TPT

But if the Spirit of Him who raised Jesus from the dead dwells in you, He who raised Christ from the dead will also give life to your mortal bodies through His Spirit who dwells in you. Romans 8:11 NKJV

He personally carried our sins in his body on the cross so that we can be dead to sin and live for what is right. By his wounds you are healed. 1 Peter 2:24

But he was pierced for our rebellion, crushed for our sins. He was beaten so we could be whole. He was whipped so we could be healed. Isaiah 53:5

For further declaration: 1 Corinthians 6:19 | 1 John 4:17

What words do you live by? Do you speak negatively about yourself and others? There is life and death in your tongue. Will you choose to speak life? Jesus tells us that we should not live by bread alone, but by every word that proceeds from the mouth of God. His words are life-giving. They bring healing and truth. Do you treasure his words more than your food? Not one word that comes from the mouth of God will return empty. Grab hold of the thread of his promises. Weave them in your life daily. Picture what he has spoken as already done. You will find that your emotions will receive healing and catch onto the truth when they hear you speak his life-giving words over yourself.

Woven Thread

Thread
It's every word you've said
Pulling on the truths
Diving in the deep
Speaking out with confidence
Bridging unseen to seen
Thread woven
Lit up with faith
Picturing it done
Father, Spirit, Son

Now faith brings our hope into reality and becomes the foundation needed to acquire the things we long for. It is all the evidence required to prove what is still unseen. Hebrews 11:1 TPT

For further declaration: Isaiah 55:11 | John 6:63 | 1 John 5:7 | Matthew 4:4

There is a hallelujah echo washing over your mind and emotions. We shift the stale. It's time to grasp the mail. Bring your heart to the Lord. Begin to thank him, joining the great multitude in heaven who are already crying out 'Hallelujah'.

A Hallelujah Echo

Crown of glory is your story
Dazzling grace upon your face
We welcome peace in this place

You carry heavens dew
Speaking out what's true
Reviving things to new
Ushering the yahoo!

Shifting the stale
Grasping my mail
Echoing hallelujah over the frail
Blessings and praise are your phrase

You can pass through his open gates with the password of praise. Come right into his presence with thanksgiving. Come bring your thank offering to him and affectionately bless his beautiful name! Psalm 100:4 TPT

After this I heard what seemed to be the loud voice of a great multitude in heaven, crying out, "Hallelujah! Salvation and glory and power belong to our God. Revelation 19:1 ESV

For further declaration: Isaiah 62:3 | Numbers 6:26 | 1 Thessalonians 5:16-18

Peace is an orgasm of the heart, the pinnacle moment that you rest in, where your heart pulsates and things slow down. Oxytocin and dopamine are released in this space of peace. It brings you to the awareness that God is close, and it is through intimacy with him that you find peace. Peace covers your mind and your heart simultaneously. Choose to step into peace as a lifestyle. Welcome Shalom (Hebrew word for peace, wholeness, completeness, tranquillity) as your long-standing guest.

Shalom

You sing over me
I wonder, what's the melody?
This heart is feeling cloudy
The mind very rowdy

I welcome Shalom
Pacman is having a nom
Yielding what was wrong
Now it's all gone

Shalom my crown and shield
A metron of rest
Not only for quests and keeping out pests
But a long-standing guest
I'm a host for this rest

Shalom my home
Thank you for making yourself known
Never leaving me alone
Exchanging rubbish for my heavenly coverage
Surpassing all understanding

My Prince of peace
Treasure forever
My guard and friend
I'll pursue you till the end

You will keep in perfect peace all who trust in you, all whose thoughts are fixed on you! Isaiah 26:3

Now, may the Lord himself, the Lord of peace, pour into you his peace in every circumstance and in every possible way. The Lord's tangible presence be with you all. 2 Thessalonians 3:16 TPT

Turn away from evil and do good. Search for peace, and work to maintain it. Psalm 34:14

Therefore, since we have been made right in God's sight by faith, we have peace with God because of what Jesus Christ our Lord has done for us. Romans 5:1

For further declaration: Ephesians 4:3 | Romans 8:6

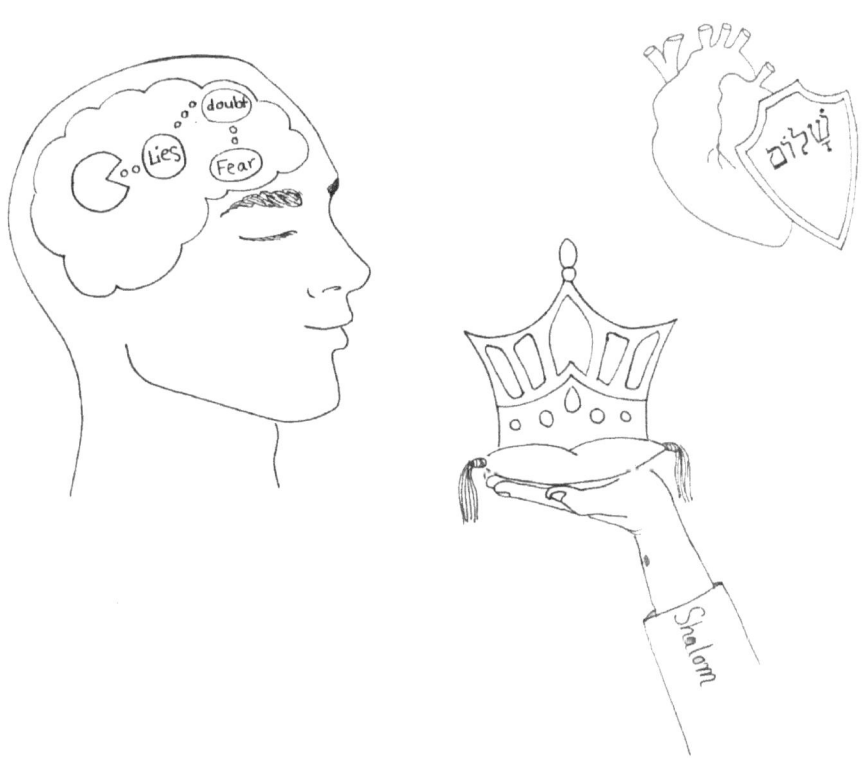

Do you know you are more valuable than the birds in the air? Come rest your tender heart. Allow the Holy Spirit to declutter the unhelpful thoughts you think about yourself. May you receive an overflow of the goodness of God.

Tender Heart

A heart that's tender
Resting in my splendour
Gleaning from my treasure
You have authority over the weather
With an abundance of all things clever
Joy is yours forever

When you see the bird's flutter
Remember to declutter
Know that you matter
More than words can utter

Keep coming to my table
I've got words for every angle
Keep shining my beautiful candle

Because I set you, Yahweh, always close to me, my confidence will never be weakened, for I experience your wraparound presence every moment. My heart and soul explode with joy - full of glory! Even my body will rest confident and secure. Psalm 16:8-9 TPT

For further declaration: John 10:10 | Psalm 31:19

For the one who struggles with telling lies or lies have been spoken to you and you have believed them. Close the door to lies today! Pinocchio has got to go. Jesus has life giving words for you to eat instead. We release a renewing of your mind. Be set free. Step into truth. God is not the author of confusion, but of peace. Who the Son sets free is free indeed! Amen.

Pinocchio Has Got to Go

Let it go, all your woe
Even all the things you don't know
Choose to silence Pinocchio
He must never star in the show
Trade with me
I'll set you free
Faith is the cradle
Eat from my ladle

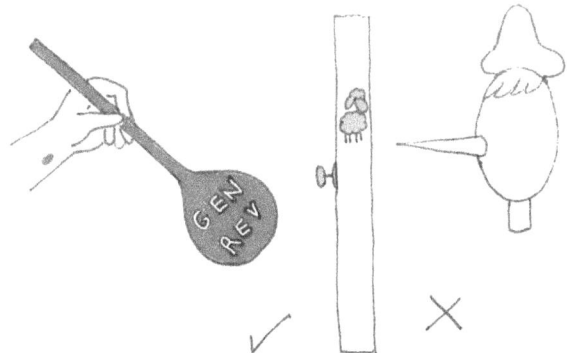

Death and life are in the power of the tongue, and those who love it will eat its fruit. Proverbs 18:21 NKJV

I have not departed from the commandment of His lips; I have treasured the words of His mouth more than my necessary food. Job 23:12 NKJV

For further declaration: 2 Corinthians 10:5 | John 8:44 | Romans 12:2

Have you felt like your path in life has been feisty? Allow these words to declare life over you. May your hope and faith increase. We declare your path has become mighty.

The Mighty Path

In the push and pull I'm breathing something new
Standing tall in this garden
Just look at the flowers, they speak of hope
They sway and dance in the breeze, like a little party!

Looking down at my feet
They've become the roots of an oak tree
Living waters nourishing me
Every leaf telling a story of victory

My strong branches overshadow the seeds
Pointing to new paths of creativity
Expanding wisdom and strategy that **go beyond me**
Leaving the seeds of legacy

A path once feisty became mighty

He will be standing firm like a flourishing tree planted by **God's design, deeply rooted** by the brooks of bliss, bearing fruit in every season of life. He is never dry, never fainting, ever blessed, ever prosperous Psalm 1:3 TPT

And the Lord will continually guide you, and satisfy your soul in scorched and dry places, and give strength to your bones; and you will be like a watered garden, and like a spring of water whose waters do not fail. Isaiah 58:11 AMP

For further declaration: Proverbs 13:22 | Isaiah 61:3 | James 1:5

You may have kept a record of all that's wrong with you, but Jesus doesn't. You are created in God's image. May you think of yourself as God does. He exults over you with loud singing. May you hear him singing over you. May songs swell, rise, and dance within you until they bubble to the surface in spontaneous praise. His thoughts about you are more than the grains of sand. They are peaceful thoughts. God is pleased with you. You are enough. Allow these words to get rid of the fluff and strengthen you.

I am Enough

This might sound strange
These words arranged
The words you've collected
Where you've been connected
Have left you depleted

Don't take the bite of self-pity
Surround yourself with the witty
Chase away the flies
That are telling you lies

You are more than enough!
It might feel tough
Get rid of the fluff

It might mean you do a loud scream
Throw out the unseen
There is light in this fight
You are strong
Get yourself a song

Go ahead - sing your new song to the Lord! Let everyone in every language sing him a new song. Psalm 96:1 TPT

For further declaration: 2 Corinthians 10:5 | Zephaniah 3:17 | Ephesians 6:12 | Psalm 40:3

There is a blessed assurance that no matter what you face, hope will pop up in its place. Allow these words to assist you back to hope.

Blessed Assurance

When I feel like I'm sinking
You are with me

When my finances are shrinking
You are with me

When sickness invades
You are with me

When loneliness shades
You are with me

When mouths ramble against me
You are with me

When lies fly
You are with me

When two hearts depart
You are with me

When identity is stripped
You are with me

When death takes
Even there you are with me

There is blessed assurance
In the endurance

No matter what I face
Hope pops up in place

The faithful love of the Lord never ends! His mercies never cease. Great is his faithfulness; his mercies begin afresh each morning. I say to myself, "The Lord is my inheritance; therefore, I will hope in him!" Lamentations 3:22-24

So let's not get tired of doing what is good. At just the right time we will reap a harvest of blessing if we don't give up. Galatians 6:9

Dear brothers and sisters, when troubles of any kind come your way, consider it an opportunity for great joy. For you know that when your faith is tested, your endurance has a chance to grow. So let it grow, for when your endurance is fully developed, you will be perfect and complete, needing nothing . . . God blesses those who patiently endure testing and temptation. Afterward they will receive the crown of life that God has promised to those who love him. James 1:2-4, 12

For further declaration: Hebrews 12:1-2 | Psalm 107:9

Is there a build-up of emotions and thoughts keeping you stuck or possibly feeling dirty? Have you been robbed of your purity? Friend, come as you are. You are safe before God. He loves you more than you can imagine and has collected every tear. We break off shame and any sense of guilt that you may carry. We unclog the constipation that is blocking your path. We release a washing over your mind where painful memories have tormented you. We release peace as a covering that surpasses all your understanding. May peace guard your heart and mind in all circumstances from now on. We release redemption over the times in life where you were caught in situations that were not of your choosing. Jesus is like a launderer's soap; he is restoring purity to you today. Yes, you are a precious treasure, and what has been robbed or stolen from you is being redeemed. In Jesus' presence you are made new. Allow these words to wash over you.

I am Made New

My body feels like a washing machine
In the soaking
In the turning
In the scrubbing
In the rinsing
In the spinning

Clearing my constipation
The dirt of lies spoken
The hurts in my emotions
The rusty reels on the screen of my mind
The buried dreams from the grit of destruction

All is washing away now
Reviving my heart
A new perspective
A fresh scent released

I am made new
It's all because of you
I come as I am

Where you greet me
Fresh every day
I have become a bubbling brook
Through every nook
My new daily outlook

He is like a refiner's fire and like launderers' soap. Malachi 3:2 NKJV

At each and every sunrise you will hear my voice as I prepare my sacrifice of prayer to you. Every morning I lay out the pieces of my life on the altar and wait for your fire to fall upon my heart. Psalm 5:3 TPT

For further declaration: 1 John 1:9 | Isaiah 1:18 | Jeremiah 29:11-13 | Hebrews 10:22-23

Life has thrown many curve balls. Maybe they happened to you, or you made some silly decisions. Jesus is removing that storm cloud as you read. We remove the regret of the past and release freedom for your next steps. The wrong narrator hijacked your story, but God is the author of love. He works all things together for good. May you receive a fresh outpouring of his love. He is so pleased with you, and his face is shining on you. God is light, and you are a child of light. We release Jesus' light to flood your heart and mind in this very moment. Jesus is lighting your path—can you see it? May he open your eyes so you can see who is for you, like he did with Elisha's servant. Innumerable angels surround you, and they are on your winning side. We release boldness, courage, and wisdom over you as you make decisions going forward. Everything you need in life has already been provided because God supplies all your needs. May your heart become tender to God's voice. Allow his words to become the soundtrack you walk to.

The Light to My Path

My tongue is a soundtrack
Enlightening the road map
Shifting life's hacks
Walk the dust and trust
For lush green is your scene

Your word is a lamp to guide my feet and a light for my path. Psalm 119:105

Keep me from the traps they have set for me, from the snares of those who do wrong. Psalm 141:9

For further declaration: Proverbs 16:9 | Psalm 23:1-3 | Romans 8:34 | Psalm 121:3

Are you bogged down in your blues? No-one would even have a clue what's going on internally, but you can feel the heaviness. Maybe you soak your pillow most nights in your sorrows. We release to you hope for brighter days ahead. This hope is anchored in the heavenly realms where love is poured out over you. Allow these words to bring renewed hope.

Renewed Hope

There's an ocean of blue surrounding you
No one has a clue what's bothering you

But you are seen
There is wisdom to glean
Your heart can be made clean
Wherever you've been

There is hope!

I see you dusting off the scruff from this ticker
You stretch out your hands
I see love poured out
Everything has already been paid for

Anchored in you
Hope made new

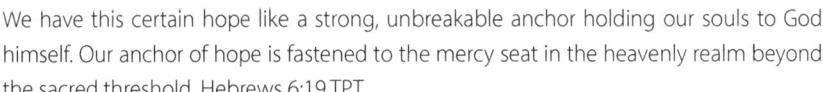

We have this certain hope like a strong, unbreakable anchor holding our souls to God himself. Our anchor of hope is fastened to the mercy seat in the heavenly realm beyond the sacred threshold. Hebrews 6:19 TPT

The eyes of the Lord search the whole earth in order to strengthen those whose hearts are fully committed to him. 2 Chronicles 16:9

For further declaration: Galatians 3:13 | 1 Peter 2:24 | Romans 5:5 | Psalm 51:10 | John 8:12

Have you been through divorce, trauma, grief or abuse? What happened to you does not define you. We silence every voice that has spoken against you. We release courage to bless instead of curse. We release joy to heal your mind and your emotions. We release freedom, wisdom, and protection over you. Hold onto integrity and shake off the dust. Today peace has become your home.

Shake the Dust

Dust the scandal off your sandal
What you faced was difficult to handle

Voices may flap and sap
Don't look at that dangerous trap

Forgive the beef
Grief turns over a new leaf

Holding integrity is where you're at
Your identity is not where you once sat

Death and life are in the power of the tongue, and those who love it will eat its fruits. Proverbs 18:21 ESV

So now the case is closed. There remains no accusing voice of condemnation against those who are joined in life-union with Jesus, the Anointed One. Romans 8:1 TPT

For further declaration: Psalm 19:14 | Proverbs 4:23, 12:18 | Matthew 5:44 | Psalm 141:3

What you are facing may press you from every side, but help is on the way, even before you finish your prayer. We release joy to dry your tears. Allow these words to bring you comfort and peace.

Help is Near

When the desperation of what you're facing
Feels like it squeezes you beyond repair

Hang on longer
Help is near

The pain you feel is not the final deal
Like old wallpaper being stripped, ready for fresh paint
There is a peel to heal

All things work together for good
Even if it's not yet understood

We live by faith, not by what we see with our eyes. 2 Corinthians 5:7 TPT

Then he said, "Don't be afraid, Daniel. Since the first day you began to pray for understanding and to humble yourself before your God, your request has been heard in heaven. I have come in answer to your prayer. Daniel 10:12

For further declaration: Romans 8:28 | Philippians 1:6 | Isaiah 65:24

Are you caught up with people who take from you, chipping away at your confidence and identity? Perhaps you've been caught up with someone in the past, and the effects of what they did and said, still linger? That damage has caused you to sabotage current and future relationships/friendships, as you try to protect yourself from hurt again. There is a brand-new start waiting for you now. Allow these words to start the process of healing your mental and emotional health. We release wisdom as you navigate your friendships and relationships. Jesus is taking you out of park and into first gear, moving you forward into freedom and the ability to trust again. May you be revitalised within.

Revitalised

Light was dim
There was no grin
Traded it in
Emptied the bin

Cut off the bark
Found in park
Goodbye to that fart
This is a brand-new start

A thankful heart
Protected from every dart
Caught up in new art
Refreshed from a swim

Revitalised within
Equipped for a win

As a dog returns to its vomit, so a fool repeats his foolishness. Proverbs 26:11

For further declaration: Philippians 2:13 | James 3:16 | Hebrews 4:12 | Romans 12:17,19

Do you feel unheard? Do you hold back sharing wisdom? Your voice is valuable and powerful, you carry life in your mouth. We expose fear and discouragement and renounce partnership with them now. We break off all the chains that have held you back and kept you silent. We release freedom and healing over your mind and your emotions. We fill you with a fresh outpouring of the Holy Spirit. You have more in you than you realise, people need to hear that wise and healing expression from you. We call out the courage within you to rise. May your eyes twinkle with life-giving light and your lips speak wise and kind instructions.

Rays

Tongue of the wise
Remove your disguise
It's time to rise
And open your eyes

Eyes of light
Twinkle bright
New height
New sight

When she speaks, her words are wise and she gives instructions with kindness.
Proverbs 31:26

I am your only God, the living God. Wasn't I the one who broke the strongholds over you and raised you up out of bondage? Open your mouth with a mighty decree; I will fulfil it now, you'll see! The words that you speak, so shall it be! Psalm 81:10 TPT

For further declaration: Matthew 6:22 | Proverbs 11:30

Do you find yourself going around in circles? Are you ready to jump off that merry-go-round? We release new insights to flick on like bright lights, bringing transformation. We release wisdom to wrap you in strength. We release another wave of love to flood your heart. We release confidence as you leave the circulating paths and walk up the highway of glory, where Jesus longs to speak to you of great and unsearchable things you do not know.

Insight

As I jump off the merry-go-round
I can hear a new sound
Steps of confidence
The warmth of love
Wisdom wrapped in strength
Bright lights of insight

Those who are wise will shine as brightly as the sky, and those who lead many to righteousness will shine like the stars forever. Daniel 12:3

I am contending for you that your hearts will be wrapped in the comfort of heaven and woven together into love's fabric. This will give you access to all the riches of God as you experience the Revelation of God's great mystery—Christ. Colossians 2:2 TPT

For further declaration: Isaiah 11:2 | Proverbs 31:21, 25-26 | Ephesians 3:12

Kintsugi has been used as a metaphor for rebuilding after tragic events such as loss, sickness, trauma, and the disruption of daily life. Kintsugi, or "golden joinery" (also known as kintsukuroi, or "golden repair") is the Japanese art of repairing broken pottery by mending the areas of breakage with lacquer dusted or mixed with powdered gold, silver, or platinum. It treats breakage and repair as part of the history of an object rather than something to disguise. The repair is literally illuminated, creating something better than the original piece. Your life is being put back together as a beautiful kintsugi. Allow these words to comfort, encourage and usher you into healing.

Kintsugi

Behind the smile there were tears for a while
Sat in devastating words gnashed by a crocodile
Dwindling away
Repeat and play
Until light shone in on the potter's clay
In the new spin, where identity wore thin
Cracks filled in
Became gold within
Raising hands up
Filling the cup
Kintsugi is found
Your love abounds
This is a new sound

For God, who said, "Let there be light in the darkness," has made this light shine in our hearts so we could know the glory of God that is seen in the face of Jesus Christ. We now have this light shining in our hearts, but we ourselves are like fragile clay jars containing this great treasure. This makes it clear that our great power is from God, not from ourselves.
2 Corinthians 4:6-7

For further declaration: Romans 8:28 | Psalm 147:3 | Isaiah 64:8 | John 10:9-10

Part Two
ENCOUNTERS

To the one who is looking for love and comfort. Find your strength in Jesus today. May the resting place of his love become the very source and root of your life. God is a gardener; allow him to tend to the soil in your life. Jesus is alive; he rose from the dead for you. Did you know you are the theme of his song? We release this extravagant love to pour into you until you are filled to overflowing with the fullness of God. Lean in and drink the astonishing dimensions of what he is revealing to you. We bless your five senses to awaken to his voice. May there be an increased awareness of his presence. Like a rose given to a valentine, Jesus has become your fragrant rose today. You are wrapped in love beyond all you can comprehend.

My Rose

You are the rain
I am the soil
Let the rain fall
Nourish me
Remove the spoil
I soak in your downpour
As your love runs deep in my core
The wind blows and flows
Your voice in it, she knows
Your revealing is close
As I drink every dose
I lean into my rose

For he sows seeds of light within his devoted lovers, and seeds of joy burst forth for the lovers of God! Psalm 97:11 TPT

For further declaration: Ephesians 3:17-19 | Psalm 34:8 | Song of Songs 2:1 | Psalm 77

To the one who has been soaking in dirt for too long. The dirt shows up as unhelpful thoughts that crowd your mind. They keep you in a place of low self-esteem and snatch the moments away that should be celebrated. Right now, there is an invitation to allow the Holy Spirit to wring out all those lies and hurts, expunging the thoughts that don't belong. In this exchange He will give you a good reason to stay and soak in his goodness. In His presence is the fullness of joy. It is the greatest place to marinate. The dirty bathwater gets drained today.

Sponges

My mind set on you, absorbing all you reveal
I'm soaking in your presence
Always bringing something fresh and creative
You wring out the dirt
New life bursts forth
I'm soaking like a sponge
Heaven comes near
All senses awakened
In this atmosphere

Ink highlighted as I seek and taste your goodness
Longing to speak to you face to face like Moses
Coming after your heart like King David
Being a close friend like Abraham
You invite me in, that's a happy win
The secret place we gather in
Like a sponge I marinate
In all that is you

God, keep us near your mercy-fountain and bless us! And when you look down on us, may your face beam with joy! Psalm 67:1 TPT

For further declaration: Psalm 97:11 | Jeremiah 33:3 | Revelation 3:20 | Psalm 73:28

Encounter a love letter from God. He is speaking these words over you today.

The Almighty's Daughter

My beautiful daughter
Remember who you are!
You are a daughter of the Almighty
Splashing joy on society
Your heart's a song breathing life on what's wrong
Hope pops up wherever you show up
You have rhythms of wisdom
You are clothed in peace
Your face glistens with beauty
Mountains move with your certainty
You are hemmed in with prosperity
You are a daughter of the Almighty

With love everlasting
The Almighty God

Gaze upon him, join your life with his, and joy will come. Your faces will glisten with glory.
Psalm 34:5 TPT

Now may God, the fountain of hope, fill you to overflowing with uncontainable joy and perfect peace as you trust in him. And may the power of the Holy Spirit continually surround your life with his super-abundance until you radiate with hope!
Romans 15:13 TPT

And I will be your Father, and you will be my sons and daughters, says the Lord Almighty.
2 Corinthians 6:18

For further declaration: Proverbs 15:15 | Matthew 17:20 | Proverbs 31:26

Encounter Jesus through practising union. Pay attention to how you sense his presence as you rest in him.

I Belong

I am merged into you like a zip

In you I breathe
In you I believe
In you I groove
In you I see
In you I am free
In you I am strong
In you I sow
In you I know
In you I rest
In you I speak
In you I laugh
In you I move
In you I drink
In you I live
In you I am one
In you it is done

I belong in you, and **you belong in me**
I am merged into you like a zip

For in him we live and move and have our being. Acts 17:28 ESV

I am the sprouting vine and you're my branches. As you live in union with me as your source, fruitfulness will stream from within you—but when you live separated from me you are powerless. John 15:5 TPT

For further declaration: Ephesians 2:13 | Nehemiah 8:10 | 2 Corinthians 3:17

Have you experienced the weighty presence of God, the 'kabod' glory, where it feels like you are a magnet drawn to the ground and becoming lead-like? It is the thickness of his presence. May you encounter God in a new way today. May you feel his presence on your body so you can recognise him in your daily life. May your heart awaken to the more of God, where truth is revealed, life is renewed, and hope is restored.

Sparks in the Making

Peace, love and joy will flow
My light will hem you in
Your magnetic power draws me in

The hairs on the body tingle from head to toe
I am painting something new
Like bubbles in a cup, you burst life

New horizons
Shadows gone for the light has shone
Fire crackling, sparks in the making
Selah, pause and reflect on that

Be enthusiastic to serve the Lord, keeping your passion toward him boiling hot! Radiate with the glow of the Holy Spirit and let him fill you with excitement as you serve him. Let this hope burst forth within you, releasing a continual joy. Don't give up in a time of trouble, but commune with God at all times. Romans 12:11-12 TPT

For further declaration: Jeremiah 20:9 | Psalm 5:3 | 1 Kings 8:11

Have you experienced liquid love—wave upon wave rising from the soles of your feet to the top of your head, hugging you within? Or perhaps a bubbling in your waistline that becomes tunes of laughter? We release an encounter that transports you to Jesus' love divine. Begin to drink from his love.

Liquid Love

I am yours and you are mine
Your secrets are divine
Revealing your heart to mine
You are sweet wine
New, living wine
No limits with time

Bubbling in my waistline
Shifting my paradigm
Singing tunes of laughter
Orchestrated by my master
My holy living wine, I love how you shine
My organs dancing with the joy you're blasting
I love you, my sweet wine

I love your sloppy wet smooches
Your oozing love is always more than enough
Refills are great thrills
My friend, you are well above any trend
You are my God-send

You sit on your throne and laugh
I echo this gift with delight
It's our favourite, to share giggles day and night
I am yours and you are mine

Let him smother me with kisses—his Spirit-kiss divine. So kind are your caresses, I drink them in like the sweetest wine! Song of Songs 1:2 TPT

Suddenly, he transported me into his house of wine—he looked upon me with his unrelenting love divine. Song of Songs 2:4 TPT

I pray that from his glorious, unlimited resources he will empower you with inner strength through his Spirit. Then Christ will make his home in your hearts as you trust in him. Your roots will grow down into God's love and keep you strong. And may you have the power to understand, as all God's people should, how wide, how long, how high, and how deep his love is. May you experience the love of Christ, though it is too great to understand fully. Then you will be made complete with all the fullness of life and power that comes from God. Ephesians 3:16-19

For further declaration: Ephesians 5:18-19 | Psalm 16:11 | Acts 2:1-13

Do you feel like obstacles are blocking your way in life? Have you experienced a peace that surpasses your human understanding? Like flour in the kitchen puffs and spreads everywhere, we release peace from the top of your head to the soles of your feet.

Canopy of Love, Clouds of Peace

You have cut down the trees
Clear path to enter
Wiped fear
Under the canopy of your love
A cloud of peace over my mind
Like flour puffs in the kitchen

You will keep in perfect peace all who trust in you, all whose thoughts are fixed on you! Isaiah 26:3

In all your ways know and acknowledge and recognize Him, And He will make your paths straight and smooth [removing obstacles that block your way]. Proverbs 3:6 AMP

For further declaration: 1 Peter 4:8 | Isaiah 4:5 | Philippians 4:6-7 | Psalm 29:9

In God's presence is fullness of joy. We invite you to see more of God. Will you look so you can see? Keep your affections on Jesus and set your mind on things above. If you don't know how to do this, begin with your imagination. It's your Creator who gives good things. See yourself delighting in them with a thankful heart.

Look Up

It's time to chill at our meeting on the hill
I've got words that are sure to thrill
Faith is the bill
Joy is your pill
I am your meal
Renewing the peel that's making you squeal
I'm singing a song to silence the bong
Look up to me
You're invited to see
The new perspective I decree

Then Moses said, "I will now turn aside and see this great sight, why the bush does not burn." So when the Lord saw that he turned aside to look, God called to him from the midst of the bush and said, "Moses, Moses!" And he said, "Here I am." Exodus 3:3-4 NKJV

I have not departed from the commandment of His lips; I have treasured the words of His mouth more than my necessary food. Job 23:12 NKJV

For further declaration: John 6:35 | Hebrews 11:1, 6 | Matthew 6:33

To the one who has been feeling glum, like a glow worm has lost its shine from its bum. We release words of wisdom and insight. A shift in your perspective is taking place. May you encounter a stirring up within you, commissioning you into something new.

Bubbling Brook

I'm stirring up a new thing
The bubbling brook is opening
Received drops of honey anointing
Heat arising—which is not surprising
When the King is near
He glides on the praises of the atmosphere

Words of wisdom are like a fresh, flowing brook—like deep waters that spring forth from within, bubbling up inside the one with understanding. Proverbs 18:4 TPT

He has anointed you, more than any other, with his oil of fervent joy, the very fragrance of heaven's gladness. Psalm 45:7 TPT

For further declaration: Psalm 22:3 | Hebrews 12:29 | Psalm 104:3 | Isaiah 43:19

Is freedom deficient in your life? Do you need refreshing? Encounter the sound waves of liberty reflecting from God's heart to yours. In his presence is fullness of joy. Allow him to propel you into joy.

Liberty

Let the living waters flow
Come to the river and bath in my love
I see your honey pouring out the pot
Your wings spread open, I'm under your wings
You're my covering!

You project your heart into the depths of me
I am the jewel fastened to your wrist
You have chipped away the old
The path is made new
Your rosy hue intoxicates me,
Encircling me with awe and wonder

You're my fan, I wait in your refreshment
You sling-shot me into joy
Your winds deliver parcels
When your voice chimes instruction
As a horse gracefully jumps the fence
Liberty is echoed.

For the Lord is the Spirit, and wherever the Spirit of the Lord is, there is freedom.
2 Corinthians 3:17

For further declaration: Psalm 91 | Psalm 104:4 | 2 Corinthians 5:17 | Malachi 3:17

Do you recognize what you're wearing? Did you know that you are clothed with power when the Holy Spirit comes upon you? Put on your threads gifted from Jesus, our Messiah. Bold power and majesty are wrapped around you. Allow the Holy Spirit to assist you. Allow him to show you the power that lives within you. He overshadows you so you can bring freedom to others. It is Jesus' love that clothes you in harmony. Through union with Jesus, you are the righteousness of Christ.

My Threads

Holy Spirit invited
Oil ignited
Dunamis the sidekick
My threads, the attire gifted from my Messiah

Strength and honor are her clothing. Proverbs 31:25 NKJV

The Spirit of God has made me, and the breath of the Almighty gives me life. Job 33:4 NKJV

For God made Christ, who never sinned, to be the offering for our sin,[a] so that we could be made right with God through Christ. 2 Corinthians 5:21

For further declaration: Isaiah 61:1-3 | Colossians 3:14 | John 14:26

Are you looking for direction? There are daily treasures to be discovered. Where do you store your treasures? Jesus is waiting for you to seek out the deeper meanings of what he says. Pay attention to the signs and wonders he sends you. May you encounter his voice in a fresh way today. We release insight for the solutions to your issues. Will you choose to store your treasures in heaven? God is faithful to fulfil his promises. They are eternal and incorruptible. We invite the Spirit of wisdom and revelation, so you may know him better. May the eyes of your heart be enlightened so that you may know the hope to which he has called you.

Discovering Treasures

Clouds thick and playful like the froth in a fluffy
Could there be messages in the wind
Coming from all directions?
The chaff has been sifted
Breathing in the whiff of your existence
Spontaneous thoughts flowing
From the source of the all knowing
Daily treasures to be discovered

God conceals the revelation of his word in the hiding place of his glory. But the honor of kings is revealed by how they thoroughly search out the deeper meaning of all that God says. Proverbs 25:2 TPT

"Do not lay up for yourselves treasures on earth, where moth and rust destroy and where thieves break in and steal; but lay up for yourselves treasures in heaven, where neither moth nor rust destroys and where thieves do not break in and steal. For where your treasure is, there your heart will be also. Matthew 6:19-21 NKJV

For further declaration: John 10:27 | Psalm 19:1 | Isaiah 30:21 | Hebrews 1:7

God is love! He sits on his throne and laughs with you. You are co-seated with him. Can you hear him knocking on the door of your heart? He invites you day and night to spend time with him in the secret place. We release the ability to hear his voice with clarity. Rest in his love. He has given you a stethoscope to put on his chest to listen to the beat of his love for you. When you lean in, may your troubles hear the songs of gladness that rise. They will be reminded how big God is. The shift in focus will deliver solutions to your problems. May your face become radiant in the glow of his love. Encounter his face that puts everything in the right place.

A Heartbeat with a Seat

In the whisper I feel the breeze
I'm gliding across the ocean with ease
There is an awakening, a colourful haze
A trail of faith
Your face is what I chase
A glowing radiance
Absorbing you, the one who is true
Let it echo in the lands crafted by your hands
Fully immersed
I'm an antenna linked into your chest
A heartbeat with a seat where we meet
Your love on repeat
Flowing to the deep
Leaning in there is always more
I'm thankful for the knock on my heart door

But you, when you pray, go into your room, and when you have shut your door, pray to your Father who is in the secret place; and your Father who sees in secret will reward you openly. Matthew 6:6 NKJV

Lord, you are my secret hiding place, protecting me from these troubles, surrounding me with songs of gladness! Your joyous shouts of rescue release my breakthrough. Psalm 32:7 TPT

For further declaration: Psalm 63:1-8 | Revelation 3:20 | Ephesians 2:6 | Hebrews 13:8

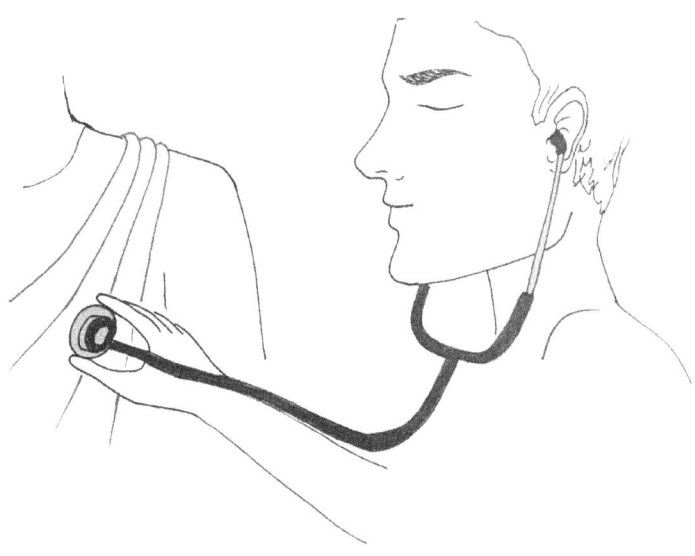

Do you want to encounter the Holy Spirit in a fresh way? Allow these words to activate something new within you.

Holy Spirit Activate

Holy Spirit awaken me, all of me

Holy Spirit activate!
Peace, Love, and Joy activate!
Patience, Kindness and Goodness activate!
Faithfulness, Gentleness and Self-Control activate!

Within me these attributes are solid
You flex, I reflect
Bliss to stay night and day

Holy Spirit activate!
Wisdom and Insight activate!
Knowledge and Understanding activate!
Strength, Counsel and Truth activate!

I am free in where you lead me
Decisions crafted, brilliance imparted

Holy Spirit activate!
Dreams, Visions activate!
Creativity, Innovation activate!

I ask the questions - you express them
Downloading awards of excellence
Delicate, distinct and precise
Filling me with diligence
Scribing the evidence

Holy Spirit activate!
Prayer Language activate!
Wind and Fire activate!

Building myself up in my most holy faith
Kept in your love
You rise up within me interceding on my behalf
Sighs and groanings too deep for words
Angels dispatched, your words matched

Holy Spirit activate!
Healing, Creative Miracles activate!
Speech, Sight, and Hearing activate!
Legs, Body, Skin activate!

Ephphatha: Open, release, loose
Instantaneous celebration containing this

Lame, paralyzed - stand up and walk!
Fully cured, fully restored
Leprosy cleansed, it disappeared, I cheered!

Your face I seek, Your heart I ask
Spiritual senses increased
Unseen realm on my lenses now
Holy Spirit activate!

Activate!
Activate!

But the Holy Spirit produces this kind of fruit in our lives: love, joy, peace, patience, kindness, goodness, faithfulness, gentleness, and self-control. Galatians 5:22

For further declaration: Isaiah 11:2 | Jude 1:20-21 | Matthew 11:5 | Matthew 8:3

Encounter the fragrance of Jesus. His sweet friendship refreshes your soul and awakens your heart with joy.

Planted and Granted

Bags of blooms
Your fragrance in all my rooms
The eagle wings are spread
Raising me up just like you said
Extending my tent pegs
A dose of your waterbed
Planted at your feet
Granted, this none can beat
The sound waves of your heartbeat
Oh, what a treat, our eyes have met

Myrrh, aloes, and cassia perfume your robes. Psalm 45:8

The Lord will guide you continually, giving you water when you are dry and restoring your strength. You will be like a well-watered garden, like an ever-flowing spring. Isaiah 58:11

Enlarge your house; build an addition. Spread out your home, and spare no expense! Isaiah 54:2

For further declaration: Psalm 1:3 | Psalm 92:12-13 | Luke 24:31-32 | Song of Songs 2:3

Are you overwhelmed and don't know what to pray? Have you tried speaking or singing in tongues? This gift keeps you in the love of God and covers you when you don't know what to pray. Its power supercharges your life, brings healing to your mind, body and emotions, and releases protection, joy, peace and much more. The Holy Spirit knows what you need and keeps you in tune with the decibels of the Almighty. We encourage you to build yourself up by doing this. If you don't speak in tongues and you want to, we invite Holy Spirit to baptise you now. We release that gift over you. Receive, and begin to speak or sing aloud the words that drop into your mind by faith. Renew your strength with the song that starts to flow from the bubble up. Can you feel it overflow from deep in your belly?

Decibels of the Almighty

Glorious one
My heart you have won
A song has begun
From the depths of me
From the depths of me

Oh, bubbling glee, flow freely
Bubble up, bubble up!

Birthing new things in the brave
The sounds and the waves make all bad things cave

Renewing my strength in the decibels of the Almighty
Looking fresh, mouths dropping, looking on like Crikey!

It's your hand you gave, it's my heart you've saved

But you, beloved, building yourselves up in your most holy faith and praying in the Holy Spirit, keep yourselves in the love of God, waiting for the mercy of our Lord Jesus Christ that leads to eternal life. Jude 1:20-21 ESV

For further declaration: John 7:38 | Romans 8:24-26 | Psalm 103:5 | 1 Corinthians 14:4

Jesus encourages you to come to him as a child. Have you seen how playful children are with their imaginary games? Have you seen how they believe you when you answer their sweet questions? They trust and believe because you are safe. They know when they ask you for a biscuit, you wouldn't give them poison to eat instead. We can learn so much from children as we come to God. Why don't you try spending time asking Jesus questions and listening for the answers. There is so much he wants to share with you. Jesus is waiting to take you on adventures. Encounter him today in open fields.

Come and Play

When you see open fields
Frolic and play

It's a vision of freedom
Let your inner child go wild

Open place for your heart space
Grab hold of fun in your run

Come and play

Jesus called a little one to his side and said to them, "Learn this well: Unless you dramatically change your way of thinking and become teachable like a little child, you will never be able to enter in. Whoever continually humbles himself to become like this little child is the greatest one in heaven's kingdom realm." Matthew 18:2-4 TPT

For further declaration: Hebrews 5:14 | Psalm 115:3

Do you remember what a shiny new car looks like? How about sparkly white teeth on an advertisement? Come and get coated in radiant glory. Get buffed, Heaven's buff!

Heaven's Buff

New beginnings
New horizons
Smothered in goodness
Coated in radiant glory
This is my every day story
Dripping with joy
Oozing with love

Heaven's buff always leaves me chuffed

The son is the dazzling radiance of God's splendor, the exact expression of God's true nature—his mirror image! He holds the universe together and expands it by the mighty power of his spoken word. Hebrews 1:3 TPT

But we all, with unveiled face, beholding as in a mirror the glory of the Lord, are being transformed into the same image from glory to glory, just as by the Spirit of the Lord.
2 Corinthians 3:18 NASB

For further declaration: Isaiah 43:19; 60:1 | Psalm 84:11 | Proverbs 25:2 | Psalm 107:9

Do you want to encounter more of God? Plunge right in. Allow these words to guide you through.

The Door

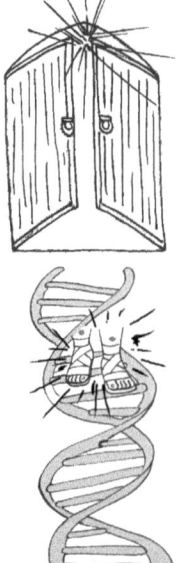

The depths
The plunge
The sponge
Something's launching
Stemming from the door that was knocking
Gliding high, led by my wise guide
Soaking up the whispers
Plunging through the mysteries
Drawing into the depths of you
Always another layer of truth
Increase in faith
Increase in love, joy and peace
Increase in favour
No need to savour
These taste buds favourite flavour
There is always more
I am the ladder, you are the open door

For he satisfies the souls of thirsty ones and fills the hungry with goodness!
Psalm 107:9 TPT

I have treasured the words of His mouth more than my necessary food. Job 23:12 NKJV

The faithful love of the Lord never ends! His mercies never cease. Great is his faithfulness; his mercies begin afresh each morning. Lamentations 3:22-23

For further declaration: Genesis 28:12 | Daniel 2:28 | Luke 2:52 | Psalm 24:7

Did you know that your name is written on the palms of God's hands? Allow him to speak to you about who you are. You were created in the image of God. God does not make mistakes. You are mysteriously complex. Encounter his love and promises today.

Promises

I look up and see stars that twinkle at me
You know them all by name

I look up and see my name written in the sky
Fully known by the living God
Before conception, that's the reason why
I am seated with you in the heavenlies
I am engraved in your palms

After the rain falls, I look up and see
A hand-picked rainbow
That echoes your name inside my frame

Bold promises proclaiming your goodness
Your voice is colourful, oh so wonderful
Your devotion kisses my heart
Thank you for eyes to see
Your promises, evidently

Whenever the rainbow appears in the clouds, I will see it and remember the everlasting covenant between God and all living creatures of every kind on the earth.
Genesis 9:16 NIV

See, I have written your name on the palms of my hands. Isaiah 49:16

For further declaration: Genesis 1:26-27 | 1 Peter 2:9 | Ephesians 1

Jesus is knocking at the door of your heart every day. Can you hear it? Perhaps you can feel it. He loves to spend time with you. He knows the struggles you go through and the help you need. He has the answers to your questions. He is inviting you to come away with him. We silence all the distraction and noise, and welcome peace. His words bring life to your body. Encounter God's voice and marinate in his bliss. Be still.

Marinate

Pull the plug
Drain the noise
Sitting poised
Listening to your spontaneous voice

Here I marinate in your quiet brook of bliss

Yahweh is my best friend and my shepherd. I always have more than enough. He offers a resting place for me in his luxurious love. His tracks take me to an oasis of peace near the quiet brook of bliss. Psalm 23:1 TPT

For further declaration: Psalm 46:10 | Matthew 6:6 | Mark 1:35; 6:31-32 | Revelation 3:20

Do you have big decisions ahead? Are you lacking wisdom and insight for situations? Are you searching for purpose or needing healing in your body? Encounter God in your dreams; it's direct mail.

Direct Mail

Weaving light all through the night
Dreams come in sight
Truth unveiled
His voice is hailed
It's direct mail for the path to entail
Visions crafted decisions
Wisdom written before the ink disappears
Reflection glistening as the keys are whistling
My incredible King is speaking
While my mind and soul are sleeping
In this slumber there is lots of colour
Each night new insight

The way you counsel me makes me praise you more, for your whispers in the night give me wisdom, showing me what to do next. Psalm 16:7 TPT

In a dream, in a vision of the night, when deep sleep falls upon men, while slumbering on their beds, then He opens the ears of men, and seals their instruction. Job 33:15-16 NKJV

For further declaration: Habakkuk 2:2 | 1 Samuel 3:8-10 | Genesis 46:2 | Deuteronomy 8:3

We invite you to encounter the voice of God today. For this encounter we encourage you to find a quiet space. Jesus asks us to come to him like a child. Simply close your eyes and imagine a door. Once you see the door on the canvas of your mind, by faith physically walk through that door. You can even physically walk through the door frame, from within the room that you are in right now. Pause there, listen. Pay attention to what's happening in your body. You might sense heat, tingles or what we like to call 'jollies', since God is joyful and playful. You might feel a gentle breeze across your face or a slight electric brush against your skin. While you are there you may start to see pictures in your mind, or a spontaneous thought will be highlighted in your mind. God is speaking, and he does this through all your senses. Receive the lion's roar.

The Lion's Roar

I hear your roar over this ancient door
The frequency and vibration pulsating through me
Armour on
Raised on a mountain

Standing firm
All the cares and worries stripped bare
Victory is here
Your voice always near

What seems bleak is no longer weak, when you speak
I receive your roar
Every day there is more

For someday the people will follow me. I, the Lord, will roar like a lion. And when I roar, my people will return trembling from the west. Hosea 11:10

For further declaration: Psalm 94:17 | Revelation 5:5 | Habakkuk 3:4 | Job 37:2

Nothing can separate you from the love of God. Pour out your tears at the feet of Jesus and encounter his endless love today. He works your story together for good. With this action of praise, he takes hold of your prayers and answers them. Can you sense Jesus pivoting towards you? As you draw near to him, he draws near to you. Receive perfume for splashes.

Pivot

A volcano erupts
It's the tears from my ducts
Splashing at your feet, where they greet and . . .

Pivot.

Beauty for ashes
Perfume for splashes

I am worn out with my weeping and groaning. Night after night I soak my pillow with tears, and flood my bed with weeping. Turn from me, all you troublemakers! For Yahweh has turned to hear the sound of my weeping. Yes! Yahweh my healer has heard all my pleading and has taken hold of my prayers and answered them all. Psalm 6:6,8-9 TPT

For further declaration: Isaiah 61:3 | Romans 8:34-39 | Luke 7:37-38, 50 | Psalm 94:17-19

Come and encounter God's presence. Be expectant to absorb love, insight, wisdom and strength, amongst many other things. He has granted you permission before His throne.

Open Doors

    I once was looking through the window
    But now I am before your throne
    Permission granted
    Your heartbeat ignited pulses of light
    Waves of insight
    Strength absorbed
    Bells ringing amongst the singing
    You whistle, sending doors open with a twinkle in your eye
    Moments of beauty for the hungry and thirsty

When he saw Queen Esther standing there in the inner court, he welcomed her and held out the gold scepter to her. So Esther approached and touched the end of the scepter. Esther 5:2

Jesus said to them, "I am the Bread of Life. Come every day to me and you will never be hungry. Believe in me and you will never be thirsty." John 6:35 TPT

For further declaration: Hebrews 4:16 | Revelation 3:7 | Proverbs 2:6 | John 4:14

Do you want to encounter God via supernatural transportation? Through a relationship with Jesus and as you delight in him, you can ask him to take you on adventures. We can trust that he leads us in truth.

Transports of Delight

You are a sweet treat
I love every time we meet
Transports of delight
You are all things bright
Illuminating light
Beaming with fright
Shimmering day and night
Dazzling colours
Brilliant lover
A beauty like no other
Quick-witted, my heart admitted
Always fresh
Giving this heart rest

I was caught up to the third heaven fourteen years ago. Whether I was in my body or out of my body, I don't know – only God knows. Yes, only God knows whether I was in my body or outside my body. But I do know that I was caught up to paradise and heard things so astounding that they cannot be expressed in words, things no human is allowed to tell.
2 Corinthians 12:2-4 NLT

For further declaration: Acts 8:36-40 | Exodus 34:29-30, 33 | Matthew 28:2-4 | Psalm 86:8

God is outside of time. He can redeem your timeline, where the pain from the past doesn't have ill effects on you anymore. He can take you through time miracles, such as time reversal, calling back lost things, time travel and time standing still. When you are in glory and repeat what God says, the soundwave in that object hears God's voice through you. Where I have written 'body part', you could replace it with the body part you are missing. There are no limits with God. Come and encounter him beyond the clock.

Beyond the Clock

There's no lid to the pot
My personal hotspot
Bubbling and flowing
I abide with the all-knowing
You are beyond the clock
Tick tock! My ever-firm rock
I've lost more important things than my sock
My missing body part, for one, what a shock!
Take me where the lost things go
I'll be calling them back, from what you show

Missing body part I know you can hear me
'Cause there's no time and distance in your glory
I'm reminded of the withered hand, time reversal story
You're made of atoms, protons and neutrons
Found inside soundwaves, just like all of creation
When I speak, I co-create
With the one who hovered, at the beginning of all time

Body part, come back!
Bring yourself near me from your cellular memory
Your will be done, on earth, in my body
As it would be, had I just walked into heaven
How good though, my newest body part grew back, hello!

Reversing time, on this body of mine
A mind boggling thought
Heaven landed with the good sort
How profound, vision and sound help the lost things come round!

Lord, you have reigned as King from the very beginning of time. Eternity is your home. Psalm 93:2 TPT

Before the mountains were born, before you gave birth to the earth and the world, from beginning to end, you are God . . . For you, a thousand years are as a passing day, as brief as a few night hours. Psalm 90:2, 4

Jesus looked at them intently and said, "Humanly speaking, it is impossible. But with God everything is possible." Matthew 19:26

How great is our Lord! His power is absolute! His understanding is beyond comprehension! Psalm 147:5

He existed before anything else, and he holds all creation together. Colossians 1:17

For further declaration: Hebrews 1:2 | John 1:1-3,14 | Joshua 10:13 | Mark 3:1-6 | Ezekiel 37

Did you know you can train your senses to hear God? Do you want to encounter Jesus through your sense of smell? He loves to commune with you. Here is an invitation to dine with him.

Honey Dew

Honey dew straight from you
Could it be a clue, or a woo?
My affection drawn to you
The scent that came and went
But in the moment it lingered
There was pause and reflect
A signal so sweet
Creates anticipation for a deeper meet

Kind words are like honey - sweet to the soul and healthy for the body. Proverbs 16:24

But solid food belongs to those who are of full age, that is, those who by reason of use have their senses exercised to discern both good and evil. Hebrews 5:14 NKJV

For further declaration: Mark 6:31-33 | Song of Songs 2:10 | Hebrews 5:14

Allow yourself to be clothed in God's wonder. He has joy for heaviness and rest for burdens. Seek his face, where new thread is graced.

Clothed in Wonder

My precious child, I clothe you in my wonder
Through every storm I am with you
In the boom of thunder
My living water flows within you
Inhale my words of life, I adore you
You're written on my palm
Orchestrated in fun
I am the wind chime
Sending you new wine
Introducing joy for your lifetime

Come dine with me
Come dance with me
Come praise with me
Come laugh with me

Child, my life and beauty are in the core of you
Each time you seek my face new thread is graced

I am overwhelmed with joy in the Lord my God! For he has dressed me with the clothing of salvation and draped me in a robe of righteousness. Isaiah 61:10

Every host serves his best wine first, until everyone has had a cup or two, then he serves the cheaper wine. But you, my friend, you've reserved the most exquisite wine until now! John 2:10 TPT

For further declaration: Isaiah 61:3 | Matthew 11:28 | Nehemiah 8:10 | Psalm 5:11

Are you looking for wisdom? Jesus is faithful to give it to you when you ask. Have you forgotten how valuable you are? Every day, Jesus is longing to spend time with you. He loves to remind you how significant you are. It is in him you will find your true worth. Allow these words to usher you back to love, hope and joy.

Shouts of Hooray

I take your hand day by day
I'm singing shouts of hooray over you!
You are my joy, my tender soil
Your garden is growing and flowing
My face shines upon you
My excellence adorns you
My sweet one, I love you

If you wait at wisdom's doorway, longing to hear a word for every day, joy will break forth within you as you listen for what I'll say. Proverbs 8:34 TPT

May the Lord bless you and protect you. May the Lord smile on you and be gracious to you. May the Lord show you his favor and give you his peace. Numbers 6:24-26

For further declaration: Psalm 25:5 | Zephaniah 3:17 | James 1:5

Do you feel side swiped, heartbroken, or are you carrying a heavy load of some sort? This battle is not yours. We release angels to war against the dark forces, to bring you freedom and the answers you have been longing for. We release joy to bubble up within you and comfort to rest over you. You have a seat at the table. You are seated and celebrated! Put praise back on your lips. Watch the jaws of the enemies drop in shock, because you have chosen to feast on the goodness of the Lord. That is an image that will cause you to chuckle even right now. Let's just pause and laugh at that on purpose! They can watch you get blessed over and over again, while they have no place at the feast. Pick up your cutlery and enjoy the banquet!

Seated and Celebrated

Valley deep
Table set
Seated
Celebrated
Enemy flabbergasted

I overflow with praise when I come before you, for the anointing of your presence satisfies me like nothing else. You are such a rich banquet of pleasure to my soul. Psalm 63:5 TPT

For further declaration: Ephesians 6:12 | Daniel 10:12-13 | Song of Songs 2:4 | Psalm 23:4-5

To the one who is in need of a faithful companion. You might be surrounded by people who chip away at your soul with negative words and exasperating insecurities. There is a faithful companion who has never left your side. His name is the Holy Spirit.

Faithful Companion

I'm sending you a kiss from heaven
Receive my Spirits of seven
Grace upon grace as you run this race
Keep coming to seek my face

Light is flowing in the atmosphere
I am your torch guiding your way
A fresh embrace
Abundance trumps haste
I'm taking the waste
I'm setting your taste

As I enthrone your praise
Something new I'll raise
Be encouraged, I'm making you flourish
I release shalom from dusk to dawn
I'm your faithful companion
Keeping you standing

Will you choose to trade for the upgrade?
Receive my thoughts
They're of all sorts
More than grains of sand that covers this land
My darling you've been given the upper hand

Sharpen your sword
Speak my word
Goodness and mercy are your chords

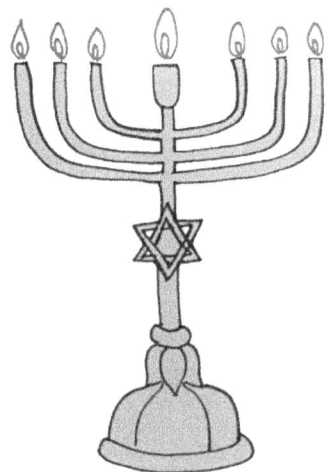

Surely goodness and mercy shall follow me all the days of my life; and I will dwell in the house of the Lord forever. Psalm 23:6 NKJV

How precious are your thoughts about me, O God. They cannot be numbered! I can't even count them; they outnumber the grains of sand! And when I wake up, you are still with me! Psalm 139:17-18

For further declaration: Romans 10:17 | Isaiah 11:2 | Psalm 68:4 | Psalm 119:105

Do you rely on your own understanding? Choose to trust the Lord. You may have troubles coming from different directions, but Jesus never abandons you. He is ready to trade with you, offering peace for the cares of your heart. It is through him that you are strengthened to do hard things. Nothing is impossible with him. Will you choose to acknowledge him in all your ways? He promises to remove all obstacles as you trust in him. We release a refreshing peace over you today that will surpass all your understanding. God is closer than the air we breathe. As you choose to yield, breathe in deeply and receive life back into your nostrils.

Living Dust

A leaf fluttering in the breeze
Crossing the high seas with ease
You always soothe my quease
Yielding all from my knees

A diamond in the rough
Ridding of the scruff
Leaning into you for my buff
I can never have enough
In you I put my trust
You make me living dust

I love you, Lord; you are my strength. The Lord is my rock, my fortress, and my savior; my God is my rock, in whom I find protection. He is my shield, the power that saves me, and my place of safety. Psalm 18:1-2

Then the Lord God formed the man from the dust of the ground. He breathed the breath of life into the man's nostrils, and the man became a living person. Genesis 2:7

For further declaration: 2 Corinthians 4:8-9 | Psalm 94:19 | Proverbs 3:5-6 | Nahum 1:7

Do you feel abandoned and ready to give up? Are you feeling stuck? Perhaps you keep waiting for dreams to unfold and promises to be fulfilled but they seem to be just collecting dust. We release to you today an increase in faith. We release new clothing to replace the old. We release encounters, where you are reminded that God is closer than the very air you breathe. His healing pours out on you today. May signs and wonders that you have never experienced before, unravel around you.

Fresh Spark

You are always in the room
You light the wick of my heart
You give me a new wardrobe of fresh spark
Whispers sending jollies down my spine
And your drink is divine
It's a full weather forecast with you
Permanent goodness
Drenched in your sweetness

I feel you, riding in on the wings of winds
Mysterious feathers appear
Reminding me your shelter is here
Hope springs up like a new flower
Your healing pours down like a shower

He will cover you with his feathers. He will shelter you with his wings. His faithful promises are your armor and protection. Psalm 91:4

You have all become true children of God by faith in Jesus Christ! Faith immersed you into Christ, and now you are covered and clothed with his life. Galatians 3:26-27 TPT

For further declaration: Jeremiah 23:23-24 | 1 Kings 19:12 | Psalm 107:1 | Proverbs 20:27

Are you reaching for deeper truth and trying to rebuild your life? This poem came out of an encounter I had with Jesus. I was deep in loss, searching for truth and all-round hurting. I was weeping in my room deep in the night while singing songs to Jesus. I wanted to feel his hug, so I cried out for one. He came into my room and hugged me. I could feel the weight of his presence on my skin. He hugged me so tight that every vertebrae down my spine cracked. Now that's what I call a good hug. I sank into his love I felt at that moment. He shifted the deep sorrow out of my heart and hope began to rise for what was ahead of me. Have you experienced a physical touch from God? We release this over you today. Allow Jesus to heal those broken spaces. There is a new song rising, can you hear it? The sound waves are flowing straight to your heart. A beat that greets your new chapter in life. A beat that brings you to your feet in exultation. We release a new structure that doesn't fracture. Grief is departing. We release joy to zap you like lightning. Within your heart there is an arousing flame. Here is your moment of suddenly, the time has come. Your future is bright.

O, the Song

Arms open wide
You don't need to hide
Heat all down my sides
As I embrace your light

No cloud-shape mysteries in the sky today
But the sound of your wooing in the breeze
The trees dancing with all their leaves
Sparks of life flowing off your tongue
As you fill my heart with every one

Surely, we are singing a new chorus
Thank you that you are for us
The wheels are turning
This engine is yearning, learning, stirring

Sound waves of *amor*
Flowing from the throne to *Mi Corazón*
O the song, O the song
The structure of my manufacturer
The cure for her as it were

Then Jesus said, "I am light to the world, and those who embrace me will experience life-giving light, and they will never walk in darkness. John 8:12 TPT

A new song for a new day rises up in me every time I think about how he breaks through for me! Ecstatic praise pours out of my mouth until everyone hears how God has set me free. Many will see his miracles; they'll stand in awe of God and fall in love with him. Psalm 40:3 TPT

At each and every sunrise you will hear my voice as I prepare my sacrifice of prayer to you. Every morning I lay out the pieces of my life on the altar and wait for your fire to fall upon my heart. Psalm 5:3 TPT

For further declaration: Isaiah 30:18 | John 14:6 | Psalm 81:10 | Zephaniah 3:17

God speaks in many ways. There are no limits. He has even caused a donkey to speak before. Can you imagine? Hee haw! It is God's voice that fills us with life, creates, causes things to happen, and so much more. Encounter the voice of God in a fresh way.

Voice of God

Come, O breath
Fill me

Awaken my spiritual senses
—to see, hear, taste, smell, and feel

Senses activate!
The time has come to recognise the voice of God

Warmth has embraced me within
Words travelling from breath to spirit
Caught up in the sound

I am tuned to your frequency
Spontaneous thoughts light up on my mind
Glimpses of pictures flash across this canvas too
When greeted with peace
A yes is decided to keep going in what is guided

When I sleep my body is resting but my spirit's awake
Receiving dreams by my Creator
Movies that speak to numerous things
Your voice is diverse, even found in the stillness and nature
Day and night you are there for me
Ready to love, lead and guide
Immanuel, you are with me
My Creator, who continues to create and recreate
Has become my best friend

The wise counsel God gives me when I'm awake is confirmed by my sleeping heart. Day and night I'll stick with God, I've got a good thing going and I'm not letting go.
Psalm 16:7-8 MSG

And after the earthquake there was a fire, but the Lord was not in the fire. And after the fire there was the sound of a gentle whisper. 1 Kings 19:12

When he speaks in the thunder, the heavens roar with rain. He causes the clouds to rise over the earth. He sends the lightning with the rain and releases the wind from his storehouses. Jeremiah 10:13

For further declaration: Psalm 29:3-9 | Numbers 22:28 | John 16:13

Do you feel alone? Are life's pressures building up and weighing you down? No matter what you go through in life you are never alone. May your eyes be opened to see who is for you. There are innumerable angels ready to help you when you call on Jesus. There is joy in the adventure the Lord is leading you on. The Holy Spirit, who is the third person of the Trinity, was sent to be your helper. He speaks of things to come. He is your advocate. He is your counsellor. We release freedom, truth, wisdom, understanding, joy and restoration over you. God's promises are true and never come back empty. Choose to abide and allow the Holy Spirit to guide.

Abide

I remain in you, continually receiving, believing, trusting

I may feel like I am falling off the horse at high speed
But I abide in my guide

I may feel like my head is dramatically just above water
But I abide in my guide

I may feel like I'm walking across a bridge with gaps within it
But I abide in my guide

I may feel alone with hard decisions to make
But I abide in my guide

I may not have a place to rest my head
But I abide in my guide

I may not have a friend to share life with
But I abide in my guide

I may have a bank account that looks like a corpse
But I abide in my guide

I may feel like all my cares are heavy on my shoulders
But I abide in my guide

I may have landed a great job
But I abide in my guide

I may have beautiful healthy children
But I abide in my guide

I may be advanced in finances
But I abide in my guide

When I have repeated many mistakes
Yet I abide in my guide

When I abide,
My guide sharpens my vision
My guide leads me in truth
My guide heals my wounds
My guide seals me as his
My guide resets my past
My guide bathes me in love
My guide brings to memory forgotten things
My guide knows all things
My guide calls me friend
My guide gives me wisdom and understanding for complex things
My guide removes my guilt and shame
My guide knows my name

No matter what I go through good or bad,
My guide is always by my side

When you abide under the shadow of Shaddai, you are hidden in the strength of God Most High. Psalm 91:1 TPT

But if you live in life-union with me and if my words live powerfully within you - then you can ask whatever you desire and it will be done. John 15:7 TPT

For further declaration: Ephesians 1:13 | John 15:4 | John 14:15-17, 26 | Isaiah 11:2

To the one who has been through deep disappointment and all the walls in your life have come crashing down. You might be wondering, how did I get here? Your emotions are thick and your eyes are sore from crying. You don't even think you could cry anymore. Maybe you blame yourself for decisions you made that led you to this place? Or maybe things out of your control just happened to you? Maybe you lost a loved one. Today Jesus wants to rebuild those walls and make you strong again. He is inviting you in to taste his goodness. He has heard your cry. He is ready to embrace you. Lean in and be dazzled by his wonder.

Spirit-kissed

I have tasted your goodness
My strong fortress
Oh what a privilege
Dazzled in your wonder
Built bridges
Removed curtains
Received whispers with sloppy kisses
Tangible squeezes
Warmth lingering as we exchange gazes
A blissful place in your ever-flowing grace

Let him smother me with kisses—his Spirit-kiss divine. So kind are your caresses, I drink them in like the sweetest wine! Your presence releases a fragrance so pleasing - over and over poured out. For your lovely name is "Flowing Oil." Song of Songs 1:2 TPT

For further declaration: Psalm 34:8 | Psalm 72:18 | Psalm 18:2 | Psalm 91:15

To the one who has been living in a leaky house. The words you have been speaking to yourself, whether in your mind or spoken out loud, have left you with leaks within, giving you a sense of emptiness. People around you have contributed to your wounds. They have snuck in unbeknown to you, and you have accepted them. Those rags were not yours to wear. We release freedom over you today. You are royalty, a son or a daughter of the Most High King. We immerse your lips in spice; from now on you will begin to speak words that give life—words that are noble, pure, true, excellent and praiseworthy. We release an Isaiah 6 moment, where a seraphim angel purges your lips with burning coal from the altar, leaving you awestruck.

Awestruck!

Birds of paradise
Sent from Christ
Lips of excellence
Immersed in spice

Canopies of love
Peace from the dove
Insight unveiled
As the nonsense is nailed

Catching a glimpse of my perfect prince
As He silenced everything that made me wince
There is more as I look in your door
From within my core I'm struck with awe!

O God, to the farthest corners of the planet people will stand in awe, startled and stunned by your signs and wonders. Sunrise brilliance and sunset beauty both take turns singing their songs of joy to you. Psalm 65:8 TPT

For further declaration: Psalm 68:35 | Isaiah 9:6, 26:3 | Philip 4:6-8 | John 14:27 | Psalm 33:8

Do you know how precious your heart is? Maybe it has been trampled on and not valued the way it should have been. Your heart is designed to be a wellspring of life. Do you know you can bless your heart by the very words you think and speak? The bible tells us that as a man thinks in his heart, so is he. We encourage you to get rid of the thoughts in your head about yourself that God doesn't have in his. You are his delight. We invite Holy Spirit to fill the chambers of your heart now. May faith arise within you. May your heart flourish like a beautiful garden as love begins to fill you and expand. We pray that you taste the fullness of joy in God's presence, and you experience divine pleasures forevermore.

Fill these Chambers

Heart I bless you
You are exquisite
You are excellent
Holy Spirit fill these chambers
There's a castle within me
The King resides here
Heart you are a beautiful garden
A place of rest
Picnics at their best
Intimate and fresh
Alpha to Omega
The red thread has woven
Heart you've been chosen
Night and Day
The roar has spoken

Holy Spirit fill these chambers
Fill these chambers to overflowing

Heart I bless you
Joy is the bunting draped over you
Love is the story you are found in

There's a private place reserved for the devoted lovers of Yahweh, where they sit near him and receive the revelation-secrets of his promises. Rescue me, Yahweh, for you free my feet from every trap. Psalm 25:14-15 TPT

You are my private garden, my treasure, my bride, a secluded spring, a hidden fountain Song of Songs 4:12

For further declaration: Ephesians 5:18 | Revelation 22:13 | Song of Songs 2:4 | John 3:16

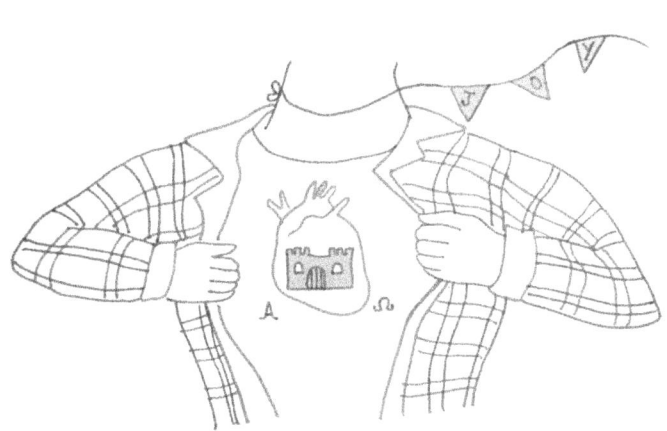

A love letter between you and your King.

My Faithful One

The Shepherd-King's child
From the cloud I can see you are proud of me

The Shepherd-King
My faithful one, I am pleased and some!
You have my "well done"
My heart you have won

The Shepherd-King's child
My Shepherd-King, I am undone by your love
You are my home

You have ravished my heart. Song of Songs 4:9 TPT

The master said, "Well done, my good and faithful servant!" Matthew 25:23

For further declaration: Numbers 6:24-26 | 1 John 4:19 | Exodus 13:21

Part Three

PHYSICAL HEALING

To the one who has an autoimmune disease, causing inflammatory symptoms. Perhaps you have rheumatoid arthritis, lupus, polymyalgia rheumatica, or psoriasis. Today your friendship with this disease is broken. Your body is being re-tuned.

Autoimmune Diseases Banished

Autoimmune, you've inflamed like a baboon
I remove the spoon where you cripple and swoon

Fatigue, you've lost your greed
I swallow a new seed

Symptoms, vanish!
You've left me famished
It is you I banish!

Bodysuit, I uproot all pain and swelling
No more insides yelling

Cells reunited
This body's decided
This body's in tune
No longer friends with the **baboon**
I'm just immune
In tune without the baboon
Given a new spoon

God spoke the words "Be healed," and we were healed, delivered from death's door!
Psalm 107:20 TPT

For further declaration: Matthew 6:9-10 | Proverbs 4:20-22 | Psalm 103:3

To the one who has mineral deficiencies in your body. No matter what your need is, God sends angels concerned with you. Angels have many different functions, and they are part of God's plan for bringing healing to you.

Flames of Fire

(Inspired by the book *Angels of Fire* by C. Smithyman)

I am a child of light
I am harnessed in the Father of lights
You have coloured flames
They sparkle bright, like Christmas lights
They each have different roles and functions
Carrying properties for restoration in my body
Breaking illnesses and diseases
Delivering body parts
Stirring up joy
Ushering in answers
Recording faith
Rapid travel
Combatting the darkness
Covering me in safety
Marked with sudden surprises
Leading me closer to you
There are many more ways
Yes, your ways, Lord
Are more than I can ask, think, or imagine
When I don't understand what is hidden
Your glory is revealed in the mysteries
It is written I even entertain angels unaware

When my need is before me
I declare and decree your words
Because your voice is within me
The flames of fire bring the words to completion

You command your angels concerning me
They are part of your plan of bringing heaven on earth
I partner with you, Almighty One

Dispatch blue flames of fire
I see an intake of copper sulphate

Dispatch yellow flames of fire
I see sodium sulphate become my mate

Dispatch orange flames of fire
I see calcium sulphate reinstate

Dispatch red flames of fire
I see lithium and strontium sulphate recreate

Dispatch green flames of fire
I see barium sulphate assist my state

Dispatch purple flames of fire
I see my rebate in copper and strontium sulphate

My mineral deficiencies are restored today
I am made whole

I will answer them before they even call to me. While they are still talking about their needs, I will go ahead and answer their prayers! Isaiah 65:24

So bless the Lord, all his messengers of power, for you are his mighty heroes who listen intently to the voice of his word to do it. Psalm 103:20 TPT

For further declaration: Psalm 29:7 | Ephesians 6:12 | James 1:17 | Hebrews 1:14

It has been a hard few years, with Covid-19 lingering around worldwide. Many people have died. People who survived this dreadful sickness have had ongoing health issues. If this applies to you, it ends today. Covid is under your feet. Your body will receive joy once again, and your very bones will vibrate with life.

Covid Destroyed

(Inspired by *Angels Of Fire* by C. Smithyman)

Covid, you have spread sickness, death and fear
But I refuse to let you take me too
Misery likes company
You won't get that from me

I am covered by a life-giving King
In his presence there is fullness of joy
The same Spirit that raised Jesus from the dead
Lives within me
He commands his angels concerning me

Lord, I ask you to dispatch blue flames of fire
Bring copper sulphate to my body
Become strength to my bones
Kill properties that hurt my immune system
Bones begin to glow

Lord, I ask you to dispatch orange flames of fire
Carry calcium sulphate from your throne to my home
Breaking all immune disorders!

Joy increase
I laugh on purpose, no matter how I feel
A sound that breaks off heaviness
Heart become merry
Sit on my countenance
You are medicine that does my body good
I am getting healthy

I will prepare something to eat
Yahweh, you surround me
You have sent your fire angels to purify my lungs
I see the glow begin to show

Yes, bones, you are glowing, you are revived
Exploding with life-giving properties from my cells
Covid destroyed
Life in abundance enjoyed

Your body will glow with health, your very bones will vibrate with life! Proverbs 3:8 MSG

For further declaration: John 10:10 | Romans 8:11 | Psalm 91 | Luke 8:54-55

To the one who has alopecia. God has numbered every hair on your head, and he doesn't withhold good things from you. What has been stolen from you will return in abundance. Begin to see your hair structure grow and repair.

Alopecia Evicted

I see the emptiness you left me with
Like a lawn mower cut you bare
Like a bank account dwindled to zero
Like a parking lot with no cars in sight
You left with a sudden goodbye

Today I speak to you, hair structure:
Grow!
Burst forth!
Flow like the breeze on the train of a wedding dress

Hair shafts, I see you sprouting up as a plant germinates
Life on each stem

I see you, scalp, fully covered
I see you like a well-groomed or manicured hedge
You have returned to me lush and graceful
Like a garland of the best flowers

Dispatch purple flames of fire
I see my rebate in copper and strontium sulphate

Hair cells, continue to grow in my hair bulbs!
You are like an endless supply of delicious treats on a smorgasbord

Alopecia, you've been evicted from this bodysuit
Goodbye, Alopecia, we will never meet again

I am a home full of growth and life
I am like a well-watered garden

A thief has only one thing in mind—he wants to steal, slaughter, and destroy. But I have come to give you everything in abundance, more than you expect - life in its fullness until you overflow! John 10:10 TPT

My child, pay attention to what I say. Listen carefully to my words. Don't lose sight of them. Let them penetrate deep into your heart, for they bring life to those who find them, and healing to their whole body. Proverbs 4:20-22

For further declaration: Matthew 10:30 | Isaiah 50:11 | Psalm 103.3 | Song of Songs 4.1

To the one who has psoriatic arthritis, gout, osteoarthritis, or rheumatoid arthritis. In this poem where it says, "Arthritis, you've been framed," replace the word with whatever type of arthritis you have. We break agreement with this disease in your body. We speak to your bones, "Receive an infusion of joy right now!" Today, arthritis is expelled from your body.

Arthritis Expelled

Bones awaken!
Receive the quaking
Behold the remaking
Creative for your taking

What's been squashed is now washed

Strengthen!
Align!
Smell the grapes in the vine

The inflamed is renamed
Arthritis, you've been framed!
Expelled from my body
Instead infused with what's jolly!

Gracious words are a honeycomb, sweet to the soul and healing to the bones.
Proverbs 16:24 NIV

A cheerful heart is good medicine, but a broken spirit saps a person's strength.
Proverbs 17:22

For further declaration: Psalm 34:20 | Proverbs 3:7-8 | Isaiah 54:17

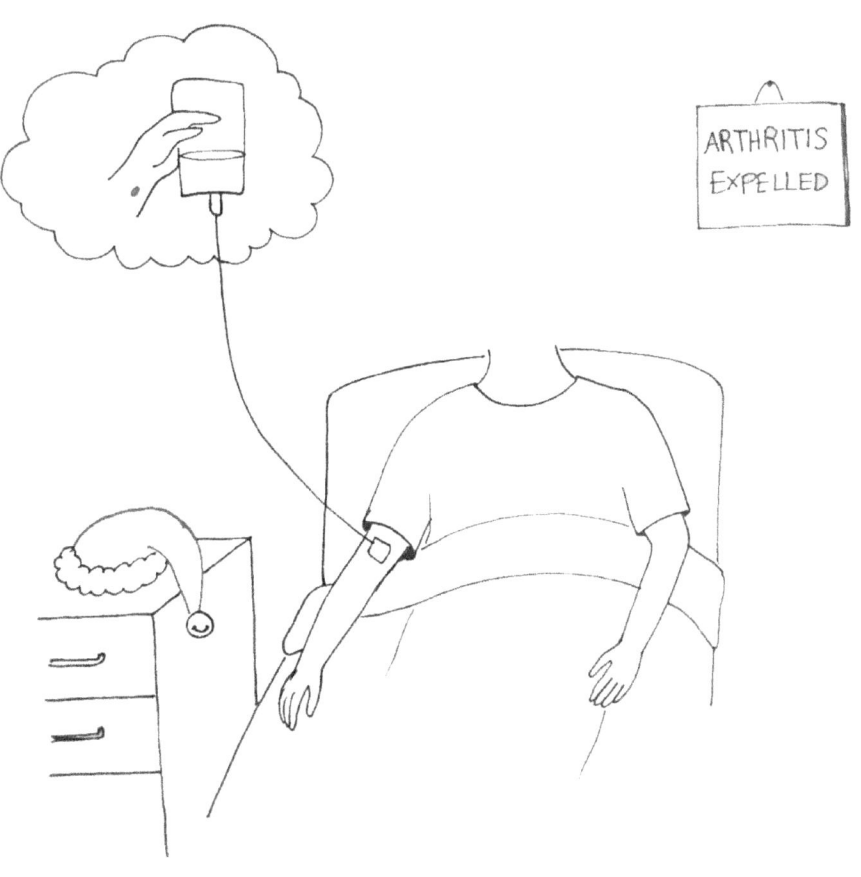

To the one who has celiac disease. We bless your body with an awakening of joy through every cell of your body. Today celiac disease has been given a spanking, extracted forever. You are carried into wholeness. Robust and cured.

Celiac Disease Extracted

Celiac disease, I reject your condition!
Diagnosis, your dictatorship ends today!
Celiac disease, you are extracted!

Jesus, come and stun me with your radiance
I am created so wonderfully complex
Body, come into alignment now!

Dispatch flames of fire
I see calcium sulphate reinstate
I see sodium sulphate became my mate
I see my rebate in copper and strontium sulphate

Bone density reset and increase!
Bones you will live!
I see you robust throughout my life's duration

Intestines, repair!
Inflammation, vanish!
Digestive system, regenerate!

I see bone marrow raise my white blood count
White blood cells annihilate viruses
Bacteria and all foreign invaders
Immune system, cheer up, protect and defend my body!

I receive your cheerful medicine today
In the wake of joy I am carried to wholeness
The display of your splendour astonishes this receiver

Shaken out
Celiac got whacked!
Joy unpacked
Cured at that!

Those who look to him for help will be radiant with joy. Psalm 34:5

You will show me the way of life, granting me the joy of your presence and the pleasures of living with you forever. Psalm 16:11

For further declaration: Matthew 21:22 | Psalm 103:3 | Matthew 6:9-10

To the one who has diabetes type 1. We encourage you to check your blood sugar levels before declaring these promises, and after too. This is so you can take note of the change. We bless your immune system and your pancreas. Today your pancreas serves you with gladness! You are made whole, my friend. Diabetes is cut off! Now walk, jump, and dance in your miracle.

Diabetes Cured

Oh pancreas, oh pancreas
You've delivered us such nonsense
The juices in my bloodstream scream: Help!

Diabetes, you shot my immune system
A hit and run, leaving me with none
Diabetes, you poach and encroach

Today I fight back!
Dispatch yellow flames of fire
I see sodium sulphate become my mate
Pancreas, you are made whole!

Blood sugar levels, I see you strong
Like a flourishing corn field
Balanced like equal weight on a seesaw
Pancreatic beta cells, release insulin now!
Liver, absorb glucose!
Glycogen, be stored in your home shaped like a dome

Cut off with the double-edged sword!
Diabetes cured!
Oh pancreas, oh pancreas
You serve me with gladness.

The Spirit of God, who raised Jesus from the dead, lives in you. And just as God raised Christ Jesus from the dead, he will give life to your mortal bodies by the same Spirit living within you. Romans 8:10-11

But he was pierced for our rebellion, crushed for our sins. He was beaten so we could be whole. He was whipped so we could be healed. Isaiah 53:5

For the word of God is alive and powerful. It is sharper than the sharpest two-edged sword, cutting between soul and spirit, between joint and marrow. It exposes our innermost thoughts and desires. Hebrews 4:12

You will show me the way of life, granting me the joy of your presence and the pleasures of living with you forever. Psalm 16:11

For further declaration: Matthew 7:7

To the one with chronic kidney disease, kidney infections or acute kidney injury. Allow these words to wash your kidneys. Today your bean-shaped organs smile within you.

Kidney Disease Flushed

Kidneys listen
You are under submission

Blood flow
Waste go

Nutrients come forth
Become a good source
Efficient filter
Rid what puts me off-kilter

Vitamins return
Hormones stay in tune

Kidneys recreate,
Look! New beans for me, mate!

There are two new beans inside
Supplied because the old were fried

Kidneys,
The two of you now smile, not stew
This body removes toxins, phew!

Heaven moved to earth for you.

He gives power to the weak and strength to the powerless ... but those who trust in the Lord will find new strength. They will soar high on wings like eagles. They will run and not grow weary. They will walk and not faint. Isaiah 40:29,31

For further declaration: Isaiah 53:5 | Psalm 103:3 | Ephesians 3:20

To the one who has a cold—a nasty, raw throat and runny nose, I suppose. Step out of the green scene. This cold has no hold on you. Imagine yourself drinking a cup of honey. Now breathe in deeply. Allow these words to sweep through your throat and nasal passages.

Common Cold has no Hold

Uvula, my fleshy extension hanging like a bell
You've begun to swell
My throat feels like a saw has cut it raw

Green has been the scene
Tissues for my issues
I've been in search of relief
To depart from this grief

Cold, your time is up!
I am handed a cup
There is a sweetness in each sip
Yip, soothing every bit!
Sweeping through
Phew, your goodness rings true

Inflammation gone
I am wrapped in a love song
My bell is in celebration
My body has become a witness

When I ask, I believe, and I receive.
A new sound is found
How profound!

Taste and see that the Lord is good. Psalm 34:8

For further declaration: Psalm 23:5 | Proverbs 17:22 | Matthew 21:22

Do you have a weak immune system? You may have a chest infection or a virus. Allow these words to reboot your immune system.

Immune System Rebooted

Wackamole is not the goal
Jesus makes me whole

Immune system, awaken
Reboot what seems taken

My angels fight the bait
Jesus sets my plate

Immune system, receive medicine from the hive
It's time to jive
The King makes me fully alive

But each **day the Lord pours his unfailing love upon me, and through each night** I sing his songs, praying to God who gives me life. Psalm 42:8

When Jesus arrived at Peter's house, Peter's mother-in law was sick in bed with a high fever. But when Jesus touched her hand, the fever left her. Then she got up and prepared a meal for him. Matthew 8:14-15

For further declaration: Psalm 30:11 | Ephesians 6:12 | Proverbs 16:24 | Psalm 91:1-4

To the one who has respiratory issues such as asthma, acute bronchitis, bronchiolitis, or bronchiectasis. Today your respiratory system is rewritten. You have been given fresh air. Your lungs are repaired. I encourage you to put your hand on your chest as you read these words.

Respiratory System Rewritten

Respiratory system, awaken and listen
I've heard your cheeky wheeze for long enough
This network cries: "Yikes,
We need wind in our pipes."

Out with the stale
Refresh each inhale

Lungs, your time has come to serve me well
With my hand on my chest, I see you revive
Lungs, recreate!
I now feel your warmth
I'm an incubator of life

Respiratory system
The new has been written
I have open pipes
Because of his stripes

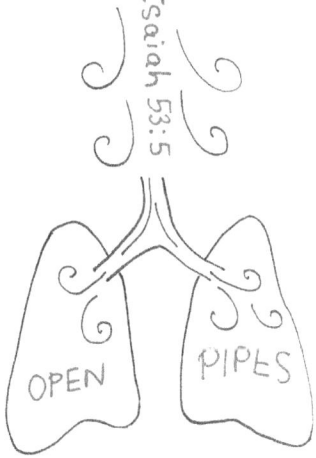

The Spirit of God, who raised Jesus from the dead, lives in you. And just as God raised Christ Jesus from the dead, he will give life to your mortal bodies by the same Spirit living within you. Romans 8:10-11

For further declaration: Mark 16:18 | Ephesians 3:20 | Psalm 77:14

To the one who is anaemic. Allow these words to catapult you into a new narrative. Today a dance has begun within you. You have an advocate who has cancelled this blood disorder. The blood of Jesus has set you free!

A Dance within Me

Iron deficiency, you've failed me miserably
Anemia, I break agreement with your intention in my body

Dispatch blue and purple flames of fire
I see my rebate in copper and strontium sulphate

I am hooked up to a heavenly IV
I begin to laugh on purpose
Joy is bubbling
Joy is a voice, a harmonious dance through my veins

Yeshua poured himself out
For me to be free

Red blood cells speak up
Oxygen flow through my blood

Blood condition, come into submission
For it is written, Jesus' blood paid for it all

I am washed
I am filled
From his blood that has spilled

Your promises are the source of my bubbling joy; the Revelation of your Word thrills me like one who has discovered hidden treasure. Psalm 119:162 TPT

For further declaration: 2 Corinthians 3:17 | John 7:38 | Ephesians 5:18 | Hebrews 12:24

Yeshua Ha Mashiach

To the one who has chronic fatigue syndrome. This is not your identity. Allow these words to whack you with joy. Today you are showered with love and infused with strength. You are held together in unity. Begin to laugh on purpose and feel the rivers of joy flow through you. Fatigue has lost its greed. Fatigue has been zapped today! Your miracle is here.

Chronic Fatigue Zapped

Fatigue you've sucked my energy with greed
On the brink of collapse, too much zinc perhaps
My daily tasks are lost in the fog of my disorientation
My cognition needs ammunition

Fatigue, I reject your existence
Holy Spirit, I accept your assistance
I speak life to my mind and body
I am hooked up to a heavenly IV
Stamina unleash within me
Whack me with joy

Dispatch blue flames of fire
I see an intake of copper sulphate

Laminin cells, regenerate muscle fibers
Laminin cells, regulate the blood in my brain barrier
Central nervous system, repair

Vitality is my frame
Shalom, you have become my home and shield
Jesus, I receive your love—wash over me

The shower of your love
Has infused me with hearty strength
I am invigorated
I am revived
I am a new creation

When I wake from sleep, I am refreshed
I have an endless supply of energy

I am a circuit of supernatural technology
I am held in unity

Jesus, in you all things hold together!

The Lord is my strength and my shield; in him my heart trusts, and I am helped; my heart exults, and with my song I give thanks to him. Psalm 28:7 ESV

The Lord sustains him on his sickbed; in his illness you restore him to full health. Psalm 43:3 ESV

For further declaration: Colossians 1:11, 17 | 1 Kings 18:46 | Habakkuk 3:4 | Isaiah 26:3

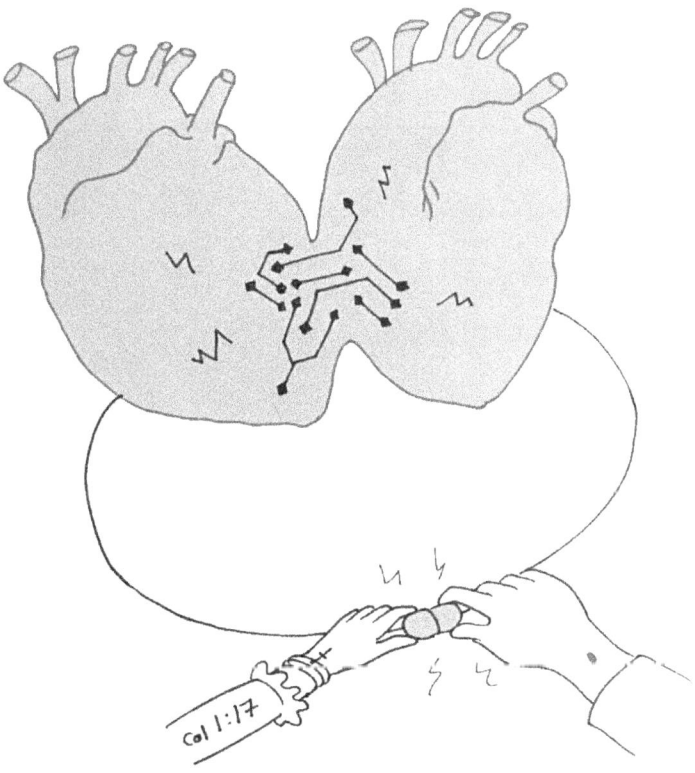

To the one who has irritable bowel syndrome or inflammatory bowel disease. Be set free today. The pest overstayed, but today we bless your bowel with words of life. Be refreshed! Receive joy and freedom in your being! Today is a new day. Enjoy living without the pest.

Living Without the Pest

Bowel, you've treated me foul
Unknot yourself now!
I feel your unravelling
Free in the travelling
No more grappling

Irritation, uplift your station!
I speak to the contraction
My body is no longer out of action!

I am smooth, in a new groove
Food brings me a new soothe

Refreshed in your best
Living without the pest!

My child, pay attention to what I say. Listen carefully to my words. Don't lose sight of them. Let them penetrate deep into your heart, for they bring life to those who find them, and healing to their whole body. Proverbs 4:20-22

Yea, brother, let me have joy of thee in the Lord: refresh my bowels in the Lord. Philemon 1:20 KJV

For further declaration: Isaiah 53:5 | Exodus 23:25 | Proverbs 16:24

To the one who has polycystic ovaries but longs to conceive. Receive your double miracle: new ovaries, and your healthy baby in your arms nine months from now. Remember to physically act on your family planning. Yes, grab your husband, close that door and . . . may life be your spread!

Life is the Spread

Polycystic ovaries, you are exposed
I oppose that this body you chose

Hormone imbalance
You are not my valance

I bring you into the light
You have lost this fight!

Red will shed
Monthly red
Unless life is the spread

Ovaries form
New life will be born

I plant the root where life can toot
Fruitful is my olive shoot

Today I step into peace

Then Jesus said to her, "Daughter, because you dared to believe, your faith has healed you. Go with peace in your heart, and be free from your suffering!" Mark 5:34 TPT

Your children will be like olive shoots around your table. Psalm 128:3 ESV

For further declaration: Exodus 23:26 | Jeremiah 32:17 | Psalm 136:4 | Matthew 21:22

To the one who has been trying to conceive and dreams of creating a family full of new life and laughter. You may have been living in disappointment while planning and waiting. Remember, you and your spouse are already a family even before bub comes along. Don't give up. I encourage you to go out and buy a baby outfit. Yes, prepare to welcome home your precious gift. Your miracle is in transition. Choose today to raise your voice and speak out your promises. God designed families, and He blesses your desires. We look forward to hearing your wonderful news nine months from now.

Knitted Together

I have been disappointed
Like a drought-filled land waiting for rain
Today I break agreement with disappointment
I now raise my voice to sing songs of victory
I speak to you dreams—come alive today!

Reproductive system, awaken
I see you fertile
Like a field producing abundant vegetation or crops

Reproductive system, nurture, develop and sustain
Both eggs and sperm
Reproductive system, you are fruitful

I am stirred with hope and resting in faith
Picturing it done
Jesus, what you have done for another I too receive
Each song I sing solidifies what has already been done

Womb, open up
Prepare your home

Womb, conceive
You are a place of life

Body, prepare, for my miracle is here

There are olive shoots around my table
I am surrounded with life and laughter

Jehovah Nissi, yes, your banner over me is love
You are faithful in all your ways
I take comfort in you
Your words never return empty

In the celebration of your love
My mouth releases thanksgiving
I have become a witness
That with you all things are possible
I am made whole, I step into peace

*Now physically join your husband or your wife and get jiggy with it.

And by faith even Sarah, who was past childbearing age, was enabled to bear children because she considered him faithful who had made the promise. Hebrews 11:11 NIV

"Sing, barren woman, who has never had a baby, Fill the air with song, you who've never experienced childbirth! You're ending up with far more children than all those childbearing women." God says so! "Clear lots of ground for your tents! Make your tents large. Spread out! Think big! Use plenty of rope, drive the tent pegs deep. You're going to need lots of elbow room for your growing family. Isaiah 54:1-2 MSG

For further declaration: Mark 5:34 | Genesis 1:28 | Deuteronomy 28:11 | John 10:10

To the one who has given birth and haemorrhoids have haunted you since, leaving you constipated, teary or uncomfortable. Or maybe you developed haemorrhoids from other circumstances. This poem is for you to get rid of the bloody thing, leaving that rear pout behind you for good.

The Pop Has Come to a Stop

Haemorrhoids, you invade like an alien
Haemorrhoids, you are a rear pout

Your constipation leaves me aching
Toxic waste, why the haste?
I just need to flow below
But you, alien, always pop out to say hello
And escape back home with a tear here and there

Haemorrhoids, no secret toot can come out your boot
Your rear pout is not the final hand I'm dealt
Haemorrhoids, you are wrong to think you belong

Inflammation, relax your hold
Pillow-like clusters of bulging veins, you are set free
Rectum and anus, strengthen your walls
Blood vessels, thin out
Irritation, leave

My canal is now free and comfy
The pop has come to a stop
No more alien invasion
Healing has come, I'm here praising

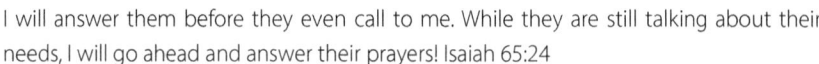

I will answer them before they even call to me. While they are still talking about their needs, I will go ahead and answer their prayers! Isaiah 65:24

For further declaration: Matthew 6:7-10 | Isaiah 53:5 | Mark 11:24

To the one who has had a unilateral or bilateral mastectomy. We release a creative miracle. What was taken from you is being restored today, precious one. After reading these words over yourself, intentionally check for change and thank Jesus.

Blossoming Bosom

Mastectomy reversed
Breasts, recreate now
Return to me healthy, fully-developed breasts
Cleavage, come into view with a superior portion
Lobes form now, surround the nipples
Like spokes on a wheel
Glandular tissue, you are no longer an issue
Areolae and nipples, adorn my breasts like a flower
I speak life over my body
What was lost is now restored
Trauma, you are broken, for joy has spoken

This is the reason I urge you to boldly believe for whatever you ask for in prayer—be convinced that you have received it and it will be yours. Mark 11:24 TPT

Because of you, I know the path of life, as I taste the fullness of joy in your presence. At your right side I experience divine pleasures forevermore! Psalm 16:11 TPT

For further declaration: Psalm 145:9 | Matthew 19:26 | Psalm 136:4

To the one who has acne or rosacea. This is not your original design. Your skin is being repaired today. Allow these words to speak life over your skin.

Traded the Pimp

Acne, all you've done is take from me

Gathered like a gang, spreading red pimps like mountains
You are uninvited
No longer causing me to hide

Bacteria and oil, stop holding your breath
These bulges I detest
You are not my original design
Inflammation, subside

Skin, repair
Skin, you are flexible
Preventing interruptions
Sebaceous glands, be restored
Release your hold
Sebum, regulate, moisturise and protect
Pores, open

Acne, you've been zapped
Skin, become my faithful organ
You have become radiant
Youthful in your glow
Scarring, I reverse time over you
No longer any trace
I have been upgraded 'cause the pimp was traded
Thank you Jesus! Fist bump, for taking each lump

He fills my life with good things. My youth is renewed like the eagle's! Psalm 103:5

If you believe, you will receive whatever you ask for in prayer. Matthew 21:22 NIV

For further declaration: Psalm 145:9 | Psalm 77:14

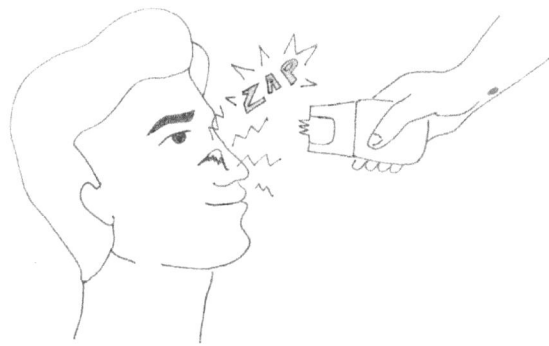

To the one who has eczema. We release a miracle across your entire body. Eczema you are overthrown.

Eczema Overthrown

Skin, revive, hydrate and thrive
You are my body's biggest organ, come fully alive!

Three layers deep, you will no longer be offbeat
Align to your original design
Eczema, you are overthrown!

Dispatch yellow flames of fire
I see sodium sulphate become my mate

This body is nourished in an oasis of bliss
Skin, nails, hair, you are stronger than a bear
Skin, you are my body's first line of defence
You must protect, direct and prevent
Blood cells and nerves, function!
Vitamin D, you are divine within me

Skin, restore!
Be cleansed!
Return to youthfulness
Integumentary system, you are radiant
To my core I'm healthy once more
No longer sore at my front door

Large crowds followed Jesus as he came down the mountainside. Suddenly, a man with leprosy approached him and knelt before him. "Lord," the man said, "if you are willing, you can heal me and make me clean." Jesus reached out and touched him. "I am willing," he said. "Be healed!" And instantly the leprosy disappeared. Matthew 8:1-4

For further declaration: Hebrews 11:1 | Psalm 77:14 | Psalm 103:5

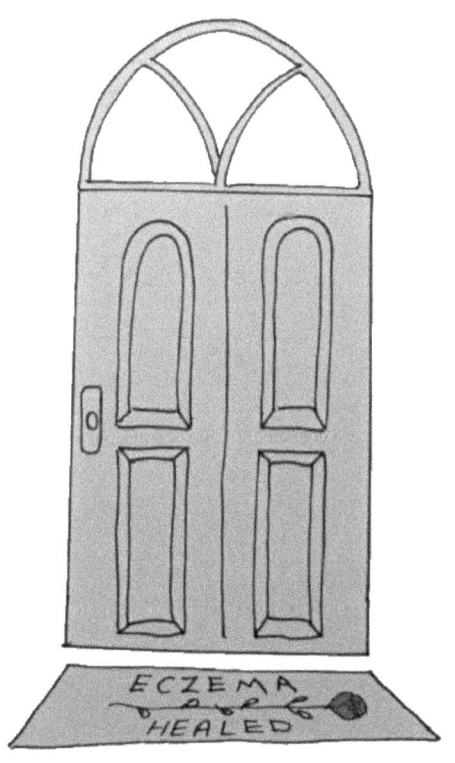

To the one who has excess weight. We release a creative miracle over you. May you marvel at the goodness of God as the weight deflates from your body and prepares a new pathway for you to live.

Obesity Deflated

Obesity, I sever your origins
You are no longer in charge
Mind, create pathways and patterns of healthy living
Metabolic system, reset!
Food you have become energy inside of me
Body, deflate excess weight!
Hands, be ready to catch knickers from this new state
Skin, strengthen and tighten at my front door
Bones and muscles, restore and strengthen
From the impact you held at base
Hormones, tune in as you sing balance right to my core
I bless you, legs and feet to carry me on repeat!
Obesity, you've got no hold on me

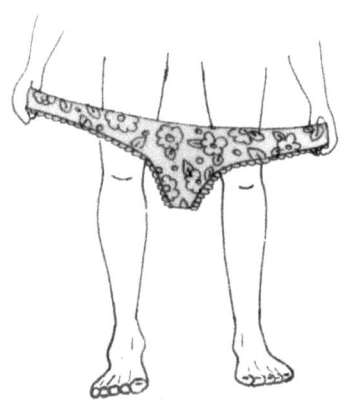

But what seems impossible to you is never impossible to God. Matthew 19:26

For further declaration: Matthew 21:22 | Psalm 139 | Exodus 23:25

To the one who dines with anger. Change your diet into a continual feast of joy. You were not designed to share your life with anger. Hold hands with liberty today. We remove the seat of destruction. Allow peace that goes beyond your own understanding to cover your heart and mind.

Cut Anger, Eat Joy

Anger, I no longer justify your presence
I see you cut off me like string
I see the prison bars open
I have stepped out of your destruction
I have broken free from your hold
My hand now holds onto liberty

Anger, I will no longer get whiplash looking at you
Your existence I cannot befriend
You no longer own me
I belong to the one who sits on mercy!
I have become wise as I clothe myself in love
I am slow to speak and quick to hear
Shalom is my new place of rest
And joy is my continuous feast

An understanding person demonstrates patience, for mercy means holding your tongue. When you are insulted, be quick to forgive and forget it, for you are virtuous when you overlook an offense. Proverbs 19:11 TPT

Set a guard over my mouth, O Lord; keep watch over the door of my lips. Psalm 141:3 NIV

For further declaration: Galatians 5:22-23 | 1 Cor 13:4-7 | Proverbs 15:1-2

To the one who has lost pigment cells in your hair follicles, causing your hair to turn grey. The hair colour from your youth is ready to return. We release a creative miracle. Allow these words to jumpstart.

Illuminated Crown

Silver and white, your presence is thick
You glisten on show the older I grow
Sparkling highlights in the midst of a glitter party

Hair, I bless you with youthfulness!
I watch with anticipation
Hair, return your glow!
I see the colours flow like an artist
Adding colour to a magnificent painting
From the sides of my temple and front to back
I receive the colour once bestowed!
I see melanin flooding in
A graceful flow that leaves my mouth open like, whoa!
Perhaps a fright with the peculiar sight

Eumelanin, rush in with abundance!
Black, you are back

Eumelanin, return your bounce with moderate tone!
Brown, you are crowned

Eumelanin, turn up like sparkling bright lights!
Blond, you respond

Eumelanin and pheomelanin, mix in like a smoothie!
Strawberry blond, you've whipped on

Across my head, pheomelanin become red!
Red, shockingly spread
I'm surrounded with joy
Every strand is grand

He fills my life with good things. My youth is renewed like the eagle's. Psalm 103:5

The Lord is good to everyone. He showers compassion on all his creation. Psalm 145:9

Give thanks to him who alone does mighty miracles. His faithful love endures forever. Psalm 136:4

For further declaration: Ephesians 3:20 | Psalm 115:3 | Isaiah 62:3 | 1 Peter 5:4

To the one who has cardiovascular conditions or diseases. You may have a pacemaker or suffer from the effects of long covid. You may have manmade heart valves. Whatever issue you may have with your heart, this poem is for you. Receive your creative miracle today.

Heart Conditions Retuned

Heart, cardiovascular conditions, and diseases
I surrender you all to the name of Jesus!
Heart, all your issues have been stink
But now I position you for something sweet

Oh, Lion of Judah, you are a skilful surgeon!
Your faithfulness and love never leave me
My treasure is in you

Positioned at your feet
Heart organs retune!
Heart, you are my home of love
Your rhythm is unique, and you regularly beat
You have a consistent and sufficient blood flow

Dispatch blue and purple flames of fire
I see my rebate in copper and strontium sulphate

My heart is no longer weary
Instead it is merry
I begin to laugh on purpose
I feel joy bubbling to the surface
A cheerful heart is good medicine

Each time I laugh, my heart praises
The name above all names
Thank you, Jesus!
Your presence is bigger than I can comprehend
You have scribed on my heart
I'm given a fresh start

Heart, you are renamed

My Creator has rewritten my circulatory system!
Each heart valve is held with strength
You have been recreated
Pacemaker, liquify!
The Lion of Judah has me equipped inside

Time has been reversed
Where past surgery left its mark
Not even a trace of any scars
I have returned to my youthful place
My heart serves me like a cheerleader

Heart organs, receive the roar!
Yes, the roar has now changed your floor
Straight from the lion's mouth
I am aligned with excellent health

Lion of Judah, your roar has made me whole
O hail, Lion of Judah!

A cheerful heart is good medicine. Proverbs 17:22

The joy of the Lord is your strength! Nehemiah 8:10

For further declaration: Proverbs 4:23 | Proverbs 3:5-6

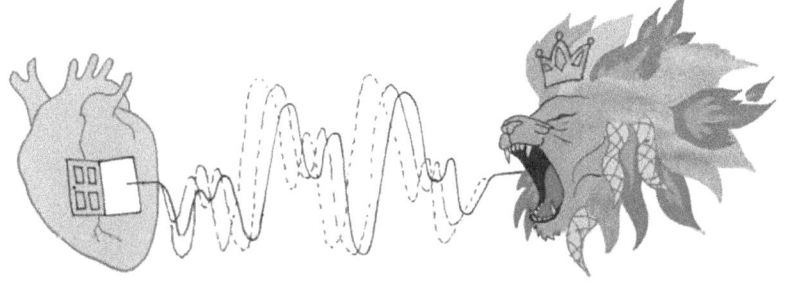

To the one who has an incurable disease. Healing is a function of the power of the blood of Jesus. Jesus' blood brings cleansing, forgiveness, mercy, justification, redemption, healing, miracles, provision, protection and much more. Jesus' name is higher than any other name. Yes, his name is higher than your incurable disease. Have your bread and red juice or wine ready to take communion with Jesus. The red thread is Jesus' blood. Choose to delight in him today. If you have not taken communion before and don't have a relationship with Jesus, there is a prayer at the back of this book. Take some time now to invite Jesus in your heart as your Lord and Saviour. Then come back to this poem.

The Red Thread Remedy

In remembrance of you
I take this broken bread
All that was said and all that was done,
You've jumbled and sent
Spread far and wide
Forgotten in the deep
Your hands wipe my tears

Fresh breath sweeps over the stale inhale
Thank you, Yeshua!
39 stripes taken for me
Sickness, flee, you are banished and silenced
Health is written in my name

I raise my cup for all that comes up
Faithful and true are you

I ask forgiveness for all my wrong
I forgive myself, and others who have struck my heart
Poison evaporates from within
You catch me as it all departs
Sending health to my mind and body

Eyes on you as you wash me through
Heart made new
Receiving love, peace and joy
This medicine I employ
Rest in my bones

Flood me with light
Communion
Fellowship with you

Jireh, my provider
Invited into your joyful union
A dance of love

The smell of rosemary rising
The sacrificed pure lamb
Your blood poured out for me
Jesus, I receive your forgiveness!

I receive your friendship!
I receive you as my Lord and Saviour!

Like a honk on the nose, a joyful pose
There is a song no matter what goes on
My heart frame is cleansed
The blood that was shed gave me life
Pausing in remembrance of you!
It's all about you
In you I stay close
I'm walking in light
I'm set in delight

For in him we live and move and exist. Acts 17:28

The next day John saw Jesus coming toward him and said, "Look! The Lamb of God who takes away the sin of the world! John 1:29

For further declaration: Ephesians 2:4-5 | Matthew 5:8 | Isaiah 1:18; 53:5 | Mark 14:22-26

To the one who has been sitting in resentment, regret and bitterness. You have stayed behind closed doors for too long. Make a choice today to forgive and be forgiven. Allow the love of Jesus to wash away the painful memories and heal your emotions. Be liberated with joy. No more hiding in the darkness. Allow love to be the clothing you wear.

The Door to Life Swings Wide

Bitterness has blinded me with lies
Resentment has tricked me into being friends
Shame has clothed me in heaviness
I have sat in torment too long
I refuse to drink from this poisonous cup anymore!

Today I choose to forgive myself for _____
I choose to forgive _____ for _____

The door has been slammed shut
On fear, shame, and regret
Trauma, like starch, has been drained out the sieve

In this moment of letting go
The door to life swings wide
I am liberated in joy!

Memories, be healed
A new pathway in my mind has begun
My heart is kept in peace
No sound of squeaky hinges
I am fully greased with the oil of gladness!

Now I am clothed in praise
I keep love on
Seventy times seven predetermines every pace
Goodness and mercy follow me all my days

Love is patient and kind. Love is not jealous or boastful or proud or rude. It does not demand its own way. It is not irritable, and it keeps no record of being wronged. It does not rejoice about injustice but rejoices whenever the truth wins out. Love never gives up, never loses faith, is always hopeful, and endures through every circumstance. 1 Corinthians 13:4-7

For further declaration: Matthew 5:44 | Isaiah 61:3 | James 5:16

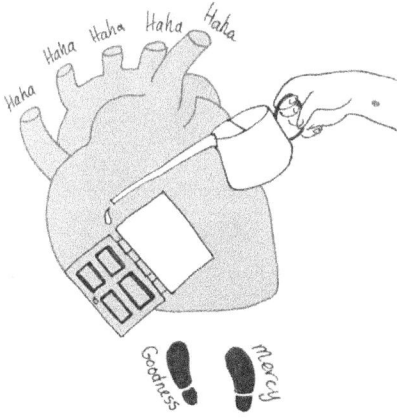

To the one who has cancer. We release a miracle over you. Body, reboot, regenerate, be cured in the name of Jesus.

Cancer Eliminated

Cancer, it's time to scoot
Body, reboot!
This disease will shriek as I speak
My life is not bleak
I am not weak
I'm watching the foreign masses shrink
Mind turn from the wink
The stink has drained down the sink

Trauma, dispose yourself in the sauna
I expose every corner

Swelling, deflate
Don't exasperate

My destiny is not infected
It has been interjected
There is wealth in my health!

This pong can't carry on
I'm singing a new song

Cancer, I see you dissolving
Like disprin hitting the water
Cancer, uproot!
You are now mute
Cancer, you are eliminated!

Fear, why do you stare?
You are not the clothing I wear

Under the stairs of my cares
My spirit cheers for the repairs
Hope is what blares

I've attached to the vine of the divine

All 37.2 trillion cells you are rewritten
Find the new rhythm
Regenerate
Revitalize
Reanimate
Reconstruct

Breathe . . .

I am cured!

Let all that I am praise the Lord; may I never forget the good things he does for me. He forgives all my sins and heals all my diseases. Psalm 103:2-3

Pray like this: Our Father in heaven, may your name be kept holy. May your Kingdom come soon. May your will be done on earth, as it is in heaven. Matthew 6:9-10

For further declaration: Luke 17:19 | Psalm 34:4 | Psalm 136:4

To the one who has leukaemia. We speak restoration into every cell, bone and organ within you. Leukaemia, you are uprooted today. Your body is a treasure that cannot wither.

Leukaemia Shrivelled

Leukaemia, your name repulses me
You are not my identity
I will stand and see victory!

Leukaemia, my body is not your home
You must shrivel up like a flower with no water

I stare you in the face, foul stench
Remove your clench!

I say nope because I have hope
My body is a treasure you cannot wither

New blood cells come forth!
All bones and organs be restored!
Body reset!

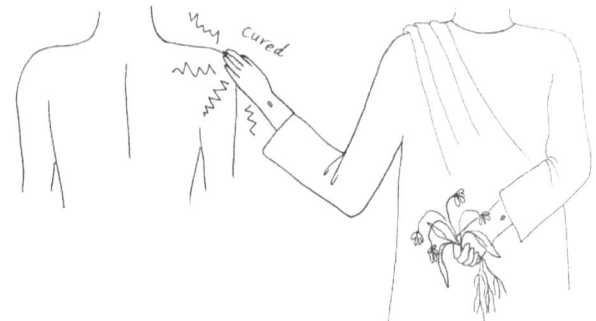

Our Beloved Father, dwelling in the heavenly realms, may the glory of your name be the center on which our lives turn. Manifest your kingdom realm, and cause your every purpose to be fulfilled on earth, just as it is in heaven. Matthew 6:9-10 TPT

For further declaration: Ephesians 3:20 | Psalm 139:14 | Psalm 30:2 | Mark 11:24

Do you have metal in your body, whether it be rods, screws, plates, fillings in your teeth, pacemakers or something else? Metal has been a temporary assistant. The true physician, Jesus the Messiah, is liquifying these foreign entities and reconstructing the areas where the metal once held you together.

Metal Liquified

Metal, you were only a temporary fix
You have been the structure, holding me
When my frame was weak
Trying to keep me from falling apart
But your foreign entities stiffen and restrict my movements

Metal, I feel you dissolve
Rods, pins, screws, plates, and bolts, liquify now!
Pacemaker, liquify!
Fillings in my teeth, be gone!

My body is heating up like the fire in a hearth
The warmth of love flowing through my body suit
Tingles and sensations waking from their slumber

I can't feel the edges, as I run my fingers along
Where you once stood
All bones on my skeleton, repair and recreate!
Nerves and muscles, reset!

My body is reconstructed and renovated
I have stepped into my original design
Body, you are made whole!

Then Jesus said to the healed man lying at his feet, "Arise and go. It was your faith that brought you salvation and made you whole. Luke 17:19 TPT

For further declaration: John 10:10 | John 20:30 | Psalm 103:2-3 | Philippians 2:13

To the one who has colour deficiency. Your eyes are designed to see vibrant colours. Allow these words to bring forth the consciousness of colour. Your colour vision awakens today.

The Eye of the Rainbow

Many colours are in view
But I wouldn't have a clue
Which one to call each of you

Colour deficiency, I break agreement with you!

Occipital lobe, connect!
Visual cortex, bring forth consciousness of colour!
Cones, come into view!
Photopigments, recreate!
Eye lenses, you are restored!

Confetti explosion is on the horizon
Shades of grey are coloured today
Hooray!

Healing retrieved
Colour received

The hearing ear and the seeing eye, the Lord has made them both.
Proverbs 20:12 ESV (emphasis mine)

For further declaration: Mark 8:22-25 | Ephesians 3:20

To the one who has cataracts. Your cataracts no longer have permission to stay. Allow these words to switch on the light. Yes, today you are being filled with light. Cataracts have been shorn and your vision is reborn. A miracle is taking place.

Vision Reborn

Cataracts, you have blurred my vision
Like unwanted dirt on the window
And, like the clouds cover a beautiful blue sky
You think you can win as you cause my eyes to dim

Today I say, "access denied!"
You are not on my side
I speak to you, cataracts
Your interference has been intercepted!
Clouds, I see new weather emerging
Scales, fall off now!
Eye lens, regenerate like a lizard gets a new tail
Eye lens, become open blinds
Be filled with light!

Dispatch orange flames of fire
I see calcium sulphate reinstate!

The veil **has been torn**
Cataracts **have been shorn**
Vision is **reborn!**

Your eye is like the lamp that provides light for your body. When your eye is healthy, your whole body is filled with light. Matthew 6:22

For further declaration: 2 Corinthians 3:16 | John 9:25 | Matthew 27:50-51 | Acts 9:17-18

To the one who has glaucoma. You are the target of God's love. Allow these words to unlock your vision once again. Your eye anatomy regenerates today. Jesus has taken back what was stolen from you. You are a child of light with restored eyesight.

Child of Light

Glaucoma, you hijacked my vision
You locked me in the dark
But I don't choose to sit in this park any longer
You cannot debate that it's too late
Because I am a child of light

Eye anatomy, listen up
Today, vision is coming back up
I bless you, eyes, with vision restored

I speak to you, aqueous humour
Provide nutrition to my eyes
Like the perfect tyre on a vehicle
You are maintained in a pressurised state

Optic nerve, recreate!
Transmit sensory information, through electrical impulses, from my eyes to brain

Eye anatomy, regenerate!
Eyes, you have become clear films
Eyes, you are light benders
Let there be light!
I receive my sight!

My eyes are the lamp to my body
My whole body is flooded with light

I am a target of God's love
I now behold the wonder and beauty around me
Glaucoma gone, yes, the light is on!
I am a child of light, restored with my eyesight

The Lord opens the eyes of the blind. Psalm 146:8 ESV

For further declaration: Deuteronomy 34:7 | James 1:17 | John 10:10 | Matthew 9:27-29

To the one who has monocular vision. This may be due to a disease process, injury, accident, or something else. As I wrote this poem for you, a vision flashed across the screen of my mind. I saw your prosthetic eye pop out and roll on the floor, while instantly a brand-new eye created and grew in its place. Today, what Jesus has revealed, he will heal. Your creative miracle is here.

Miracle Shock

Monocular vision
I've made a decision
To believe and receive
A new eye

I hear a sudden pop!
My prosthetic eye just rolled by
What a shock of drop and roll
I hear the sound of, "lol" (laugh out loud)

Eye, I retrieve you from heaven
I place you in the open socket space
Eye create!
Replace
Giving me two eyes on this face

My vision is restored
This miracle I applaud
In your name, Jesus

Now faith is the substance of things hoped for, the evidence of things not seen. Hebrews 11:1 NKJV

I tell you, you can pray for anything, and if you believe that you've received it, it will be yours. Mark 11:24

For further reflection: Mark 10:51-52 | Psalm 119:18 | Revelation 1:7 | Proverbs 20:12

Have you lost your sense of smell or were you born without it? Allow these words to send sweet smells up your nasal passages. To help activate your healing, intentionally smell something and breathe in deeply after reading this poem. Your sense of smell is awake; go and celebrate your gift!

Smells of Victory

Olfactory system
In this moment, be recreated!
Pathway, open up!
Send the sweet smells up
Whiff my way
Return to me this sensory
A gift I accept
Though you may raise a stink every now and then
At least I'll know you are fully functioning
But today you will be kind to me
With smells of victory

I am convinced that my God will fully satisfy every need you have, for I have seen the abundant riches of glory revealed to me through Jesus Christ! Philippians 4:19 TPT

For further declaration: Matthew 21:22 | Ephesians 3:20

To the one who has either short-sighted or long-sighted vision. We release a creative miracle over you today.

Apple of the Eye

Glasses, your windows and frames have become outdated
You served me when my eyes debated
Today I depart from you
I believe for something new

Myopic condition, you are rewritten
Cornea, reshape!
Lens, recreate!
Eyeball, downsize!
Light rays, bend on my retina
Myopic condition, you will not be missed
Full vision has kissed

Ephphatha: Open up
Faraway objects delightfully play
Thank you, Jesus, for the display
My world has unfurled in a new way
I am the apple of my Maker's eye
Brand new sight
My vision is bright

Hyperopia, you are rewritten
Cornea, adjust your curve
Eyeball, grow!
Light rays, come out from behind
Hit the target directly on my retina
Hyperopic condition, you will not be missed
Full vision has kissed

Ephphatha: Open up
Close up objects delightfully play
Thank you, Jesus, for the display
My world has unfurled in a new way
I am the apple of my Maker's eye
Brand new sight
My vision is bright

 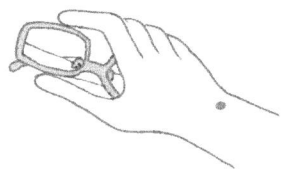

For all of God's promises have been fulfilled in Christ with a resounding "Yes!" And through Christ, our "Amen" (which means "Yes") ascends to God for his glory. 2 Corinthians 1:20

For further declaration: Psalm 17:8 | John 9:25 | Mark 7:34-35

To the one who has macular degeneration. The Lord does not withhold good things from you. He created your eyes to see. Receive your sight today. It is a good day for your miracle.

Macula, You are Spectacular

Macula, you have worked hard
You have caused my centre vision to fall apart
Whether wet or dry, my retina knows why
Blurred vision and deterioration are far from amazing

But I have remembered
The Lord created eyes to see
I will bless the Lord, oh my soul
I will not forget all his benefits!

He satisfies me with good things
In Him my youth is renewed like the eagles

Macula, I reject your distortion
Macula, regenerate!
Vision, sharpen!
Lipid, build up, drain, and go!
Nerve cells, rods and cones
Become brand-spanking new!

Eye anatomy, you are radiant
Photoreceptor cells, awaken
Play your dancing lights
Forming images that bring delight

Retina, capture the incoming photons,
Retina, transmit chemical and electrical signals
Brain, perceive the visual images

The Lord gives sight to the blind
I receive my sight in the name of Jesus!

I consider you faithful
Your promises show me you're able
I was blind but now I see!
My Shepherd rescued me
His rod comforts me
He withholds no good thing from me
Macula, you are spectacular!

"I don't know whether he is a sinner," the man replied. "But I know this: I was blind, and now I can see!" John 9:25

Bless the Lord, O my soul; And all that is within me, bless His holy name! Bless the Lord, O my soul, and forget not all His benefits: Who forgives all your iniquities, Who heals all your diseases, Who redeems your life from destruction, Who crowns you with lovingkindness and tender mercies, Who satisfies your mouth with good things, So that your youth is renewed like the eagle's. Psalm 103:1-5 NKJV

For further declaration: Hebrews 11:11 | Psalm 23:4 | Psalm 146:8 | Psalm 84:11

To the one who has a baby with lip-tie. Perhaps your infant is not latching when feeding from the breast or bottle and it is causing problems for you both. This ends today! Allow these words to loosen your baby's lips. We release a creative miracle today.

Untied

Lips, you are the entrance of nutrition
Oral tissues, loose your grip!

I see your freedom, like a kite in the wind
Labial frenulum, provide stability!

Lips, your connection has been renewed
You now have the ability to nurse from mum

Latch, sweet one
Intake the comfort of your meal

Babe, the weight you gain is healthy on your frame
With my lips I declare you are healed!

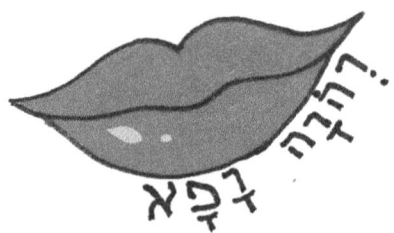

So is my word that goes out from my mouth: It will not return to me empty, but will accomplish what I desire and achieve the purpose for which I sent it. Isaiah 55:11 NIV

You made all the delicate, inner parts of my body and knit me together in my mother's womb. Thank you for making me so wonderfully complex! Your workmanship is marvelous - how well I know it. Psalm 139:13-14

For further declaration: Isaiah 65:24 | Matthew 21:22

Lip Tie Testimony

In February 2022, a young mother, who will remain anonymous, called me on the phone one Thursday. She had found an unusual lump on her breast and was having trouble breastfeeding her new-born. She had booked in with the doctor for a check-up on the following Wednesday. I blessed her, and after we hung up, I recorded myself saying a prayer for her that she could listen to in her own space. On Wednesday, the day of her appointment (and six days after we spoke), I sent her a message to let her know I was praying for her. I received a reply saying she had been referred for a scan at the end of that same week. I didn't hear back from her until four days after her scan. On Sunday, she explained that she had replayed the recorded prayer a few times during the week and had felt at peace and been encouraged to keep faith for her healing. She noticed through the week that changes had taken place. When she went for the scan, the specialist couldn't find a lump on her breast. My friend just stood there gobsmacked. The lump had vanished! She was so thankful that Jesus had healed her.

You can imagine the excitement we both shared at this moment. But wait, there's more! Other things took place that week too. First, the young mum's midwife discovered that her baby had lip-tie. So, the baby was booked in for surgery at the end of the week. This was an answer to prayer because she wanted to breastfeed her baby and needed answers. Well, you guessed it, I offered to bless her baby on that phone call and read a poem I had written for healing lip-tie. I then recorded my poem and sent it to her to play over her baby knowing that during the previous week the recorded spontaneous prayer was helpful and powerful for her to listen to and marinate in. We were believing Jesus to do it again, but this time for her baby. On the day of the baby's surgery, I messaged her again. At this point it was five days since I had read the poem over her baby. This beautiful mother called me the same day to tell me more fantastic news. She said that her baby had three consultations with three different specialists that week to be sure that surgery was the right decision. During the final appointment, the doctor concluded that her baby didn't need surgery because they couldn't find the lip-tie anymore. The baby was healed and is feeding well now. Mother and baby are happy and healthy. Praise Jesus for his healing power over this sweet baby and beautiful mother!

To the one who has a tongue tie. You may have a baby whose tongue is restricted, affecting the ability to feed effectively. If you are an adult, you may have an issue with tongue mobility. You may experience speech issues or the inability to breathe through your nose, causing you to mouth-breath. You may get frequent cavities, gum inflammation, or other oral health problems. Tongue-tie can also be a cause of sleep apnoea. Allow the words of this poem to improve your quality of life. Today your tongue will be a consistent assistant to all your needs. We release a creative miracle now.

Extend Your Tether

Frenulum linguae, you are anchored too tight
Loose your grip!
Extend your tether!
Grow!

Difficulty broken
Ease embraced

Tongue, I see movement as you facilitate
You greet my taste
You assist when I swallow
You deliver my speech

Tongue, you are a mass of muscles covered in strength
Tongue, you are my consistent assistant!

Then, looking up into heaven, He sighed and said to him, "Ephphatha," that is, "Be opened." Immediately his ears were opened, and the impediment of his tongue was loosed, and he spoke plainly. Mark 7:34-35 NKJV

For further declaration: Psalm 34:8

To the one who has a stutter or stammer affecting your flow of speech. Allow these words to catapult you into joy. Today your tongue has become a gift of speech, like a rudder on a boat steering you in a wonderful direction.

Tongue, Be Loosed

Like halloumi in its cheeky squeak
Is how I feel when I speak
You cause me to stretch as my brain plays fetch
The ick of your stick tries to snuff out my wick

Stutter, your nervous utter is about to unclutter
Hesitation is not my station
I break free from frustration
Tongue, be loosed!
Speech, your fluency is released with clarity
Tongue, you are smooth when I put you to action
My flow of speech is without a screech
My lifestyle is witty, no longer sticky
My communication runs smooth like a relaxing vacation
What a treat to enjoy this gift to speak

Concealed in your affection
Healed through your wonder
I am gathered lumber
You are the fire
Faith is the choir
I've gained speech to inspire

Open your mouth wide, and I will fill it with good things. Psalm 81:10

She speaks with wisdom, and faithful instruction is on her tongue. Proverbs 31:26 NIV

For further declaration: Ephesians 3:20 | Deuteronomy 9:3 | Psalm 136:4

To the one who has dementia. We release a creative miracle over your mind. Cognition, you are reawakened today.

Cognition Reawakened

Dementia, you have lingered too long
Dementia, you don't belong
Cerebrum, restore and awaken!
Cerebrum, initiate and coordinate movement
86 billion neuron cells, repair and grow!
Entorhinal cortex, recreate now!
Hippocampus, you've returned the springs in my mattress
Welcome back, memory (snap fingers)

I have multiple simultaneous attention
I have divided attention
I have selected attention
My cognition is flexible
My cognition is functioning
And fully alive!
Brain, you are recreated
You serve me with joy

O Lord, my healing God, I cried out for a miracle and you healed me! Psalm 30:2 TPT

The thief does not come except to steal, and to kill, and to destroy. I have come that they may have life, and that they may have it more abundantly. John 10:10 NKJV

For further declaration: 2 Timothy 1:7

To the one who has dyslexia. We release a creative miracle to rewire your brain right now. I can see Jesus doing this with a knife and fork. You have been found in a fresh mind, from scattered to ordered. Confidence has landed on your face. The very word 'dyslexia' has become displaced.

Dyslexia Expelled

Dyslexia, you are expelled!
Rewiring is now found
In every, sight, thought and sound
Yes, brain, the new wire is the new hire
Dyslexia who?
No more jumbled nonsense, poof!
Watch me read and speak with confidence
I am found with a fresh mind
Thank you for the rewiring
This original design is where I now dine!

I know what it means to lack, and I know what it means to experience overwhelming abundance. For I'm trained in the secret of overcoming all things, whether in fullness or in hunger. And I find that the strength of Christ's explosive power infuses me to conquer every difficulty. Philippians 4:12-13 TPT

For further declaration: Exodus 4:11-12 | Romans 12:2

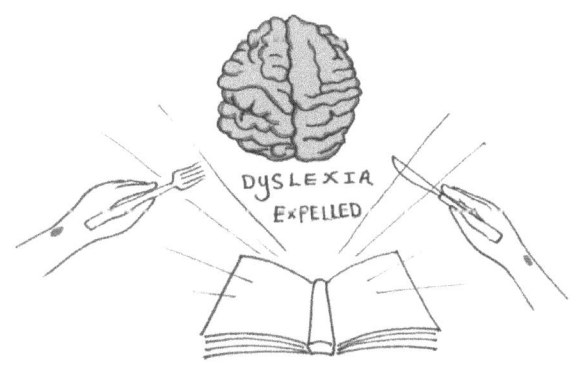

To the one who suffers from headaches of all forms. We severe the origins of the headaches. You are a medical miracle.

This Noggin Lacks Nothing

Headaches of all forms
Cluster, sinus, tension, and migraine headaches
Who do you think you are,
Causing dysfunction in my daily tasks?
You have robbed me of my peace
No surprise, you are cousins with the thief!

I am connected to the Good Shepherd
I have been given a satisfying life
Yes, life in its fullness is mine
So, I speak to you, headaches: Flee from me!
The chain of your hold is broken
All triggers have been interrupted
Stress and anxiety are now expired
I send you to the pit of hell
Peace is what I inhale
And joy is the parcel at my door

Sleep disruption, there's no exception
The promise is given:
He gives his beloved sleep
From now on I receive this quality sleep
Hormonal changes, you have been exchanged
I have clothed myself in the Lamb that was slain
In him I am dressed by original design
All hormones inside me are realigned
I am fearfully and wonderfully made!

All root causes of these aches
Have been pulled and overruled!

Intense throbbing, you've been caught robbing my home
No more, I say
You cannot stay
I smack you and send you on your way
You can't stand against me
My God is for me!

Heightened sensitivity to light, sound, and smell
You have been repositioned
No longer coming at me left-field
Your problems have been solved
I call heaven to earth
As I call, my God goes before to answer
I am replenished
In Him, it is finished!

Nausea, you poached my endorphins
It's an illegal steal
I've sent my appeal
Been rendered the verdict
Stamped and sealed
Now divine health is revealed!
I get to hoard dopamine and oxytocin
You get to watch merry sit on my face
A glowing visit
My countenance has been reimbursed!

Dehydration, a lack in my drinking
You affect my blood pressure
I am restored as I fill myself with life-giving water
Distribution of fluids to hydrate
Reawakening strength and wellbeing

Nerve damage, I declare a repair
Inflammation of membranes
Lining my brain and spinal cord
Your irritable flare-up has shifted from bruised to smooth
Your three-layered membranes protect my cord
A cord not easily broken!

Vitamin deficiencies
Jesus has the answer for all of these
Jesus, dispatch your coloured flames of fire
Adjust each deficiency, I require
Copper, calcium, strontium, sodium, and lithium sulphate

Neck and head trauma, your time has come to an end
You are cured by the name of Jesus!
This noggin lacks nothing!

Poor posture, you have put unnecessary strain
On my muscles
Neck, shoulders and back, I need a comeback!
Tension gone, strength come on
Welcome back to vitality!

Blood sugar levels, your fluctuations
Lead to spasms of the arteries in my head
You cause temporary vision-loss
Blood sugar levels, get in line!
Eye muscles, strengthen!
Vision, come into focus!
Neurologists won't know how to swallow this, gulp

Nervous system, you serve me well
This noggin lacks nothing!
I am a medical miracle!

The Lord is my shepherd, I lack nothing! **Psalm 23:1 NIV**

For further declaration: Philippians 4:7 | Psalm 30:2 | Psalm 34:19 | Psalm 91:3 | Mark 11:24

To the one who has flat feet, lacking arches. We release a creative miracle now. May the evidence be happy feet.

Happy Feet

I close my eyes and breathe in **deeply**
I am filled with peace
A covering rests over my mind **like a shield**
Feet, you are no longer flat
Arches are rising now
Discomfort gone
Balance is formed

I rise to my feet
New walk is adorned

You saw the substance
You answered with yes and **amen!**

Oh, precious are my feet
The places they greet
The evidence is happy feet

Peter and John went to the Temple one afternoon to take part in the three o'clock prayer service. As they approached the Temple, a man lame from birth was being carried in. Each day he was put beside the Temple gate, the one called the Beautiful Gate, so he could beg from the people going into the Temple. When he saw Peter and John about to enter, he asked them for some money. Peter and John looked at him intently, and Peter said, "Look at us!" The lame man looked at them eagerly, expecting some money. But Peter said, "I don't have any silver or gold for you. But I'll give you what I have. In the name of Jesus Christ the Nazarene, get up and walk!" Acts 3:1-6

For further declaration: Philippians 4:6-7 | Romans 10:15 | Psalm 103:20 | Hebrews 11:1

To the one whose ear or ears are stopped, or you have a cochlear implant. Today your ears open. You are orchestrated in a fabulous design. We release a creative miracle. Life has changed gears; you are found with beautiful, functioning ears.

Beautiful Ears

Beautiful ears
What a great pair you are
Too long you've been kept on pause
Restricting my sense of hearing to zilch

Ears don't just decorate the sides of my head
Fulfil your purpose
Open up, beautiful ears!
Create what's missing!
Recreate my middle and inner parts!

Ears, come into order!
Pinna, collect and chute sound waves
Filter and amplify through my funnel -shape gateway
Auditory canal, play the acoustics
Hit the drum, Ba-da-boom-boom!

Eardrum, vibrate!
Send and deliver to hammer, anvil and stirrup
You are like legs walking
Walk through the oval window
Set up and push pressure waves in the snail-shaped bone
Ride through
Vibrations transform into electrical energy
Stereocilia, stimulate frequencies
Travel the complex pathway to brain
I see an orchestrated order!

Ephphatha, I sigh . . .
I lick my fingers

I stick them in my ears
Change gears
Open!
Unlock!
Unstop!

Deaf ears, unblock!
Become accessible to sound
Unstopped just dropped
A sudden pop, like a cork from a bottle of wine

Cochlear implant, liquify!
Cochlear, recreate!
Become new and great
Play your key role
Snail-shaped bone, come into existence
You're a spiral with a purpose

Open up, open up!
Beautiful ears, awaken
Beautiful ears, welcome to the world of sound
You are a great pair
I can now clearly hear

Beautiful ears, I love your repairs
I'm orchestrated in a fabulous design
I've taken back what is mine
Heaven's door is open for me

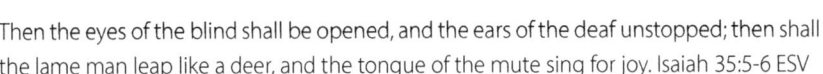

Then the eyes of the blind shall be opened, and the ears of the deaf unstopped; then shall the lame man leap like a deer, and the tongue of the mute sing for joy. Isaiah 35:5-6 ESV

For further declaration: Mark 7:32-35, 37 | Luke 11:9-10

To the one who suffers from tinnitus. Allow these words to greet you with healing. Today the high-pitched ringing has been sucked out of your ears just as a vacuum cleaner rids the house of dust. Your ear anatomy is restored. A miracle is taking place.

Ditch the High Pitch

Tinnitus,
You ring, you buzz, and hiss
I've had enough of this!

Tinnitus, your diagnosis
Has been given its notice
I ditch this high pitch!

Auditory pathways, be recreated!
Hair cells, be made new
Vestibular system, correct my balance
Repair the three-loop canals in there

I place my hands on my ears
Leaning to you, Lord, with all my cares
Knowing your word kicks into action
When placing hands on the sick
I speak your healing to my auditory system
Heat comes to meet me
A greeting of healing snuggling in
Screeching volume starts to reduce

Be still!
Be free!
Be open!

No more cacophony accepted!
My ears function accurately
Tuned in without ringing within
I receive peace in my home

Ring, buzz and hiss are sent to the abyss!
I rest in silence,
An alliance without high-pitched shares
Thank you for designing my ears!

Ear anatomy, your intricate details operate successfully
I am set free, hearing clearly
It's now quiet for me, yippee!

The hearing ear and the seeing eye, the Lord has made them both. Proverbs 20:12 NKJV

For further declaration: 2 Corinthians 3:17

To the one who suffers with scoliosis. We release a creative miracle over you today. Your bones are being restored. Do not lean on your own understanding. Long live your bones.

Long Live These Bones

Scoliosis, you are curving me sideways
Like the sound of timbeeeerrrr, a tree falling down!
It is very unpleasant to lean and dip
Scoliosis, it was not I that chose this
I am not meant to bend this way

This bending needs mending
I don't accept this bad deal
You must leave me for real
Spinal deformity, enough is enough!
I fix my eyes on Jesus
Heaven is close
In him I move, I live and have my being!
I see him moulding and reshaping my spine

Bones, awaken from your sleep!
Metal rod on my spine, liquify!
Vertebrae, recreate and reposition all five sections
Cervical, thoracic, lumbar, sacrum, and coccyx
Return to the soft 's' shape within me
Allow an even distribution of weight
And flexibility of movement

Discs in my vertebrae, I call you to do your part
Function, align and reabsorb fluid each night
Long live these bones!
Joy, come and dance in them
Surrounding muscles and ligaments, strengthen!
Allow flexion and extension

Let all that is within me praise the Lord
Yes, every bone praise the Lord!
I see the reshaping taking place
There is evidence to embrace
I feel the warmth of love circulating within me
In this new order I have become taller
My skeletal frame just became strong from maimed

I can bend low
I am repaired
I am free
I can function properly
These bones have quaked!

Scoliosis, you've got a new diagnosis!
Gone from bowed to straight
Vertebrae, It's time to celebrate
My miracle is here, I declare!
I am kept in peace

Let all that is within me praise the Lord
Yes, every bone, praise the Lord!

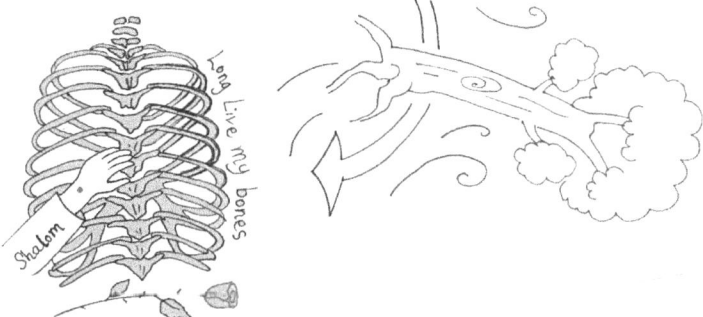

Every valley shall be exalted and every mountain and hill brought low; the crooked places shall be made straight and the rough places smooth. Isaiah 40:4 NKJV

So I prophesied as I was commanded; and as I prophesied, there was a noise, and suddenly a rattling; and the bones came together, bone to bone" Ezekiel 37:7 NKJV

For further declaration: Psalm 103:2-3 | Acts 17:28 | Proverbs 17:22 | Proverbs 3:5-8

To the one who is restricted to a wheelchair due to paralysis from an accident, chronic condition, or disease. Be healed in the name of Jesus, Amen.

New Story

Paraplegia has been my station
Sitting on wheels day to day
My spinal cord disrupted the normal flow of go
This paralysis caused loss of sensory and motor function
My legs and trunk became dormant in my story

Being a paraplegic has felt like my identity
A spark of hope has shown
This does not define me!
God works all things together for good
I consider Jesus faithful
He is more than able to get me out of this chair!

I speak to you, thoracic and lumbar spine:
Be restored!
Be made new!

Spinal cord and nerves, recreate!
Spinal cord, serve me as an information super-highway
Relay messages between my brain and body
Limbs and body, receive motor signals from brain
My spinal cord has reconnected
My nerves have become telephone lines

I have been given life in abundance
I will live it to the fullest
By faith I buy a pair of shoes
I'm getting out of this chair today!

Trauma, break off me!
I prophesy to these bones

As I rise, my bones gather together
Cracking and rattling into place

All muscles, tendons and ligaments strengthen
God you are good, so, so good to me!
I see you doing a new thing

In the name of Jesus, I leave my chair and walk!
I am a book that hasn't been written
My spine is now strong
I am off the shelf
Today I begin a new story!

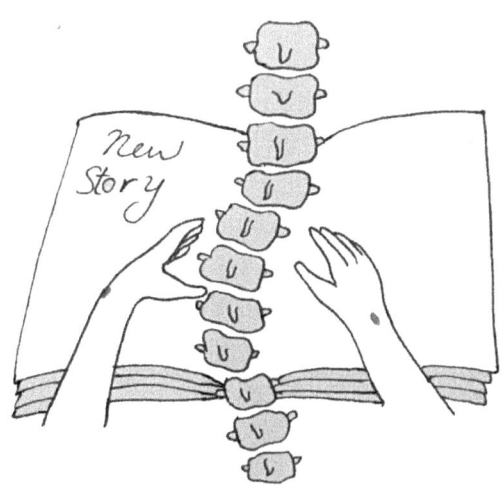

Behold, I will do a new thing, Now it shall spring forth; Shall you not know it? I will even make a road in the wilderness and rivers in the desert. Isaiah 43:19 NKJV

But Jesus looked at them and said to them, "With men this is impossible, but with God all things are possible." Matthew 19:26 NKJV

For further declaration: Acts 3:1-8 | Hebrews 11:11 | Psalm 107:1

To the one who is restricted to a wheelchair. We declare a creative miracle over you. We see you rise out of that chair. It is a good day for a miracle.

Miracle Gear

Quadriplegia has kept me in a chair
My spinal cord distorted my flowing connection
This paralysis caused loss of sensory and motor function
My arms and legs have gone to sleep

I will not park myself here any longer!
With God all things are possible!
Today I will witness something beautiful!

Lord, you are the vine I am the branches
Travel through my spinal canal
Adjust, reset, create, and recreate!
Wake up, dry bones!
Gather and repair!
Let my branches walk and cheer!
I'm getting out this chair!

I prophesy to you, body
In the name of Jesus, the Messiah,
Get up and walk!
I can feel you coming together
Each rattle, crack and pop is changing life as I know it!
Let all that is within me praise the Lord!
I can hear you singing, Let us come together
Taking me out of park and into my miracle gear

All five sections of vertebrae recreate and reposition:
Cervical, thoracic, lumbar, sacrum and coccyx
Cervical spine, support the weight of my head
Thoracic spine, help my mid-back function
Hold my rib cage to protect my heart and lungs

Lumbar spine, bear weight of my body
You are large and strong
Absorbing the stress of lifting and carrying heavy objects
Sacral spine and coccyx, become robust
Anchor and hold together with my pelvis

Spinal cord, become an informational super-highway
Relaying messages between my brain and body
Limbs and body, receive motor messages from brain
My spinal cord has reconnected

Spinal nerves become like telephone lines
All thirty-one pairs recreate!
Carry messages back and forth
Between my body and spinal cord
Control sensation and movement
Motor and sensory fibres recreate!

Intervertebral discs, cushion and separate each vertebra
Keep my bones from rubbing together
Discs, function like coiled springs
Discs, you are designed like a radial car tyre
Annulus, form your crisscrossing fibrous bands
Like tyre tread
Pull the vertebral bones together
Against the elastic resistance of the disk nucleus
Nucleus, recreate, you have become a gel-filled centre
You are like a tyre tube
Nucleus, act like a ball-bearing when I move
Discs, reabsorb fluid during each night
All muscles, tendons and ligaments strengthen

Lord, you are the vine, I am the branches
You have travelled through my spine
Adjusted, reset, created and recreated
My branches, both legs and feet
Rise to walk today

With my arms and hands,
I lift them up in praise
There is nothing you can't repair
I cheer because I'm out of my chair!

The Lord your God in your midst, the Mighty One, will save; He will rejoice over you with gladness, He will quiet you with His love, He will rejoice over you with singing.
Zephaniah 3:17 NKJV

For further declaration: Luke 5:17-26 | John 15:5

To the one who has a lung disease such as chronic obstructive pulmonary disease, asthma, acute bronchitis, bronchiectasis, or pneumonia.

Love is in the Air

I see you, lungs, receiving breath like a balloon inflating air
Expand and circulate the oxygen I need in there
The two of you are in sync
Inhaling and exhaling in a fine rhythm
I hear the sound Yahweh in the rise and fall of your breath
You are speaking a beautiful name
Fearfully and wonderfully made is this body I stand in
In every breath I find rest with your name upon my lips
Love is the very air I breathe

God is love. 1 John 4:7 NIV

For the Spirit of God has made me, and the breath of the Almighty gives me life. Job 33:4

For further declaration: Revelation 1:7 | Genesis 2:7 | Isaiah 54:17

To the one who has Parkinson's disease. We release a creative miracle. You are remarkably cured.

Remarkably Cured

Parkinson's, you have crept into my life
Progressively trying to take over
Falling over and misplacing things
Have become a regular occurrence
Life is getting slower as my movement has reduced
My coordination is losing out too
Tremors appearing
I wonder, Is there a song to go with this rhythmic shaking?
Beans—it's a word I hear a lot
The speech therapist repeats it
To increase the volume I speak
I giggle at this weird request

Parkinson's,
Your neurological disorder has caused a loss of dopamine
You have deprived me of my brain's rewards
Doctors say there is no cure
But I know the true Physician,
In him I lack nothing!

This is not God's best for me
His plans for me are good
I cancel every word spoken
That digs in its teeth to kill
Instead, I will only swallow
Words of life as my meal

Holy Spirit, plug me into your electricity
Zap this disease from me
Bodysuit, be restored!
You are wonderfully complex

Nervous system, regenerate!
Tremors and shakes, be still!
Brain, regenerate!
Rewire everything that's required!
Neurons, create dopamine
Return my brain's rewards
Stimulate movement and coordination

I speak peace over my brain and body
I breathe in your peace
Holy Spirit, fill me to overflowing!
Renew my youth
I step into your truth
I am set free!
Remarkably cured

You satisfy my every desire with good things. You've supercharged my life so that I soar again like a flying eagle in the sky! Psalm 103:5 TPT

For further declaration: Ephesians 6:10 | 2 Timothy 1:7 | Ephesians 3:20 | Psalm 30:2

To the one who has one leg shorter than the other. You may suffer from back pain due to this issue. As you speak these words to your body, your legs will align with each other. You may physically feel a sensation of pulling. You could describe this as a really good stretch. You may find a warm sensation over your leg.

Balanced

(This poem was inspired by my personal experience)

Leg, grow!
Bones, align!
Muscles, strengthen!
Back pain, leave now!
I am strong
My legs are balanced
Thank you for the new spring in my step
Amazing power received this very hour
Stretched out, without a doubt
Leg restored as whole as the other
Now let's be honest, I stand astonished!

You can ask for anything in my name, and I will do it, so that the Son can bring glory to the Father. Yes, ask me for anything in my name, and I will do it! John 14:13-14

And He entered the synagogue again, and a man was there who had a withered hand. So they watched Him closely, whether He would heal him on the Sabbath, so that they might accuse Him. And He said to the man who had the withered hand, "Step forward." Then He said to them, "Is it lawful on the sabbath to do good or to do evil, to save life or to kill? But they kept silent. And when He had looked around at them with anger, after being grieved by the hardness of their hearts, He said to the man, "Stretch out your hand." And he stretched it out, and his hand was restored as whole as the other. Mark 3:1-5 NKJV

For further declaration: John 16:24 | Psalm 6:2

Leg Lengthened Testimony

In 2006, I was playing rugby at high school. I got tackled while I was looking at my coach who was calling out from the side-line. The force impacted my hip and I felt the nerves shock my leg. The pain was excruciating. I ended up with a hip labral tear for seven years. It caused me to limp and left me with grinding of the hip, numbness, and discomfort day and night. In 2013, a couple prayed for me, and as I went to stand, I nearly fainted. I was lightheaded from the power that went through me. All the pain left my hip instantly. I was able to walk and sleep with no pain. I still had a small limp, although I didn't notice it much. Fast forward to 2019; I was in a gathering with some people from the School of Faith and I asked a couple of ladies to pray for my leg to grow. Voila, my leg grew to the same length as my other leg, approximately one centimetre! It felt like a really good stretch in my leg, and a warm sensation all over. I drove home that night with the heat still there. My leg muscles were strengthened overnight. Since this experience I haven't had lower back pain because my legs are aligned. Between 2020-2022 I have prayed for five people who have received leg growth or realignment.

Getting to Know Jesus

Dear friend,

God loves you passionately. He desires to have a living relationship with you and to give you salvation, purpose, and eternal life. Choosing to walk with him is an important decision that only you can make. Romans 10:9 says: "If you openly declare that Jesus is Lord and believe in your heart that God raised him from the dead, you will be saved."

If you would like to begin a personal relationship with Jesus today, pray this prayer out loud:

> Jesus, I believe you died for me, that your blood paid for my sins, and you rose from the dead for me. Jesus, I ask for forgiveness for all I've done wrong. Thank you for dying for me, forgiving my sins, and giving me the gift of eternal life. Today I invite you to come into my heart and life. I receive and acknowledge you as my Lord, Saviour, and friend. I choose to trust and follow you. Holy Spirit, fill me with your love and joy. Guard my heart and mind with your peace in the mighty name of Jesus, Amen.

Congratulations, precious one! I am so excited for you. You have just made an important and very wise decision. Luke 15:10 says there is joy in the presence of God's angels when even one sinner repents!

I encourage you now to find a group of people who love and follow Jesus as you continue your journey. I also suggest you purchase a bible from a local Christian bookstore or download one of the many bible apps available.

Author's Note

In 2017, I was in a place of brokenness. I had left an abusive relationship and taken my two young children to safety, where we started all over again. I turned to Jesus and asked Him to heal me so I could raise my children as a healthy mother, and enjoy life again, knowing who I am and my purpose in this world. I prayed this because my identity had been stripped from me amongst all the ugliness I had encountered. I left the relationship with an injury inflicted by my ex—a 3.5mm tear on my radial collateral ligament, at the elbow joint. I was going to need surgery to fix it. But as I stood in a church service singing praises, all of a sudden, I felt heat come over my arm. All the pain and swelling vanished instantly. This was a miracle. God's love healed me. At this time, I heard Holy Spirit say, "earnestly desire the spiritual gifts" (1 Corinthians 14:1).

Immediately, I started having a desire to read the bible, studying every healing and miracle that took place. Alongside that, I began researching and studying books on healing, miracles, prophecy, wisdom, seeing in the spirit, discernment, angels, and much more. I would invite the Holy Spirit to counsel and teach me what I needed to know, and how to start seeing these things in my life, the lives of my children, and in the world around me.

I remember crying in my room one night when everyone was in bed. That night, I began singing to Jesus, releasing all my deep hurts. As this was happening, I sensed someone had walked into the room. I didn't see anyone with my physical eyes, but I tangibly felt a giant bear hug where every bone in my spine cracked. Now that's what I call a good hug! Love began to fill my heart. Jesus loved me back to life.

In January 2019, a lady I knew broke her toe. This was confirmed on X-ray. When I went to visit her, she tripped over a chair that someone had left in the middle of the room, and stubbed her already broken toe again. She was in terrible pain. I felt compassion for her, so I asked if I could pray for her toe. She agreed. We didn't see immediate change; however, she went and had another X-ray taken, to check how the toe was tracking. The doctor reported the bones were healed! She came back to visit me a week later, wearing shoes. We were so excited! God is so good. This was one of the first healings, through my hands and partnership with God, that I had seen take place.

In July that year, I joined the School of Faith—an online school that teaches the curriculum from Bethel School of Supernatural Ministries in Redding, California. I am currently a revival group leader within the school.

One day during a gathering at the school, I was given a prophetic word about writing. Right away, I felt an unusual sensation of someone scribing across my heart. It was tangible; I physically felt it, but it was also supernatural. Sometime later, a friend gave me another prophetic word that was a piece of paper with handwriting on it. As soon as he spoke those words out, I got zapped with electric currents right through my body, followed by spinning movements for thirty minutes. I must have looked like a washing machine! "Haha"

After that, I began to write each day. Holy Spirit was healing me emotionally as I expressed my heart on paper. The power of words became very evident, and my writing pieces turned into poetry. The love of Jesus poured out—he was downloading love letters! Poetry became a language of healing for me, a place where I could hear God speak, revive, and restore. Alongside these poems, wherever I went, I was already praying for miracles where people needed them. I expanded my writing, and these poetic remedies found in this book, emerged.

God speaks, and He continues to speak words of life that bring healing and miracles to our lives. His heart is for you. He entrusted me with these remedies to share with you. I pray my testimony brings you hope that God is writing a beautiful story of your own. He is working all things together for good.

With love,

Penelope J. Kern

Final Words

I trust that you have enjoyed reading Poetic Remedies, and that you have stepped into healing, miracles, love, joy and peace in a fresh way. I would love to stay connected. Please reach out to me via email penelopej.kern@gmail.com to share how this book has impacted you. I encourage you to get a medical report from your doctor showing the documentation of your healing before and after. What Jesus does for you, he can do it again for another. Your story is powerful. Also, if this book has blessed you, please write a review on Amazon. You can also find me on Instagram:

@pennydrop_ | @penelopekern

Bless you as you continue your journey.

Penelope J. Kern

About the Author

Penelope J. Kern is a revival group leader with School of Faith, an online Supernatural School delivering BSSM Redding, California curriculum. She is a passionate revivalist, gifted in discernment and in prophetic and healing ministry. Her desire is to see people walking in a deep relationship with the Lord and operating in the gifts to see their lives transformed. Longing for all to discover that God is good, Penelope helps people hear the voice of God and step into the freedom that Jesus paid for. Penelope lives with her two beautiful children in Wellington, New Zealand.

www.ingramcontent.com/pod-product-compliance
Lightning Source LLC
Chambersburg PA
CBHW062033290426
44109CB00026B/2618